Fitness Weight Training

Second Edition

Thomas R. Baechle

Roger W. Earle

Human Kinetics

Library of Congress Cataloging-in-Publication Data

Baechle, Thomas R., 1943-
  Fitness weight training / Thomas R. Baechle, Roger W. Earle.-- 2nd ed.
    p. cm.
  Includes bibliographical references and index.
  ISBN 0-7360-5255-0
  1. Weight training. 2. Physical fitness. I. Earle, Roger W., 1967- II. Title.
  GV546.B33 1995
  613.7'13--dc22

                                        2004024500

ISBN-10: 0-7360-5255-0
ISBN-13: 978-0-7360-5255-9

Acquisitions Editor: Ed McNeely; **Developmental Editor:** Leigh Keylock; **Assistant Editor:** Kim Thoren; **Copyeditor:** Robert Replinger; **Proofreader:** Darlene Rake; **Indexer:** Betty Frizzéll; **Permission Manager:** Carly Breeding; **Graphic Designer:** Nancy Rasmus; **Graphic Artist:** Tara Welsch; **Photo Manager:** Dan Wendt; **Cover Designer:** Keith Blomberg; **Photographer (cover):** ©Royalty-Free/Corbis; **Photographer (interior):** Dan Wendt, unless otherwise noted; **Art Manager:** Kareema McLendon; **Illustrators:** Mic Greenberg, Kareema McLendon; **Printer:** Versa Press

We thank Body Tech in St. Joseph, Illinois, for assistance in providing the location for the photo shoot for this book.

Human Kinetics books are available at special discounts for bulk purchase. Special editions or book excerpts can also be created to specification. For details, contact the Special Sales Manager at Human Kinetics.

Printed in the United States of America   10 9 8 7 6 5 4 3

Human Kinetics
Web site: www.HumanKinetics.com

United States: Human Kinetics
P.O. Box 5076
Champaign, IL 61825-5076
800-747-4457
e-mail: humank@hkusa.com

Canada: Human Kinetics
475 Devonshire Road, Unit 100
Windsor, ON N8Y 2L5
800-465-7301 (in Canada only)
e-mail: orders@hkcanada.com

Europe: Human Kinetics
107 Bradford Road
Stanningley
Leeds LS28 6AT, United Kingdom
+44 (0)113 255 5665
e-mail: hk@hkeurope.com

Australia: Human Kinetics
57A Price Avenue
Lower Mitcham, South Australia 5062
08 8372 0999
e-mail: info@hkaustralia.com

New Zealand: Human Kinetics
Division of Sports Distributors NZ Ltd.
P.O. Box 300 226 Albany
North Shore City, Auckland
0064 9 448 1207
e-mail: info@humankinetics.co.nz

There are some special people who inspired us and supported us, and whose influence has enabled us to accomplish far more than we ever imagined, including the completion of this second edition of *Fitness Weight Training*. To them, we dedicate this book:

Our wives and children:
Tom's: Susie; Todd and Clark
Roger's: Tonya; Kelsey, Allison, Natalia, and Cassandra

Our family and friends:
Tom's: Walter and Elnora, Betty and Allen, and Tom "Smooth" Burkhardt
Roger's: Linda and Larry, Bryan and Brandon, and David Potach

Contents

Preface   vi
Acknowledgments   viii

PART I
Preparing to Weight Train

1 Weight Train for Fitness   3

2 Know Your Equipment   9

3 Check Your Weight Training Fitness   17

4 Make a Successful Start to
  Your Program   23

5 Set Up Your Program   27

6 Weight Train the Right Way   39

PART II

Training By the Workout Levels

7   Muscle Toning   55

8   Body Shaping   75

9   Strength Training   105

10 Weight Training Exercises   139

PART III

Designing Weight Training Programs

11 Design Your Own Program   191

12 Combine Weight Training With
    Aerobic Exercise   199

13 Weight Training for a Sport   205

Appendix   213
References   218
Index   219
About the Authors   223

Preface

In this section of the previous edition of *Fitness Weight Training*, we wrote about the desire to use our talents in ways that would make the greatest contribution to others and how writing the text provided a vehicle for us to do that. Since that edition was published, *Fitness Weight Training* has sold over 102,000 copies and has been translated into four languages. Our goal to reach thousands and to provide them with research-based weight training programs that would improve health and fitness was realized. Writing this new edition provides an opportunity to make an even greater contribution to improving the quality of life for many.

Many times, we have discovered that one of the largest roadblocks a person experiences when beginning a weight training program is simply not knowing what type of program to follow. For anyone who steps foot in a large fitness facility, high school or college weight room, or even the sporting goods department of a retail store, seeing the many different types of machines and equipment can be instantly intimidating. Even if you have previously weight trained, figuring out how many sets and reps to perform and how much weight to lift can be overwhelming.

The purpose of this book is to break through these barriers by providing you with

- a method to allow you to determine your initial weight training fitness level;
- information and questions to help you set a specific exercise goal;
- photographs and technique guidelines for 41 weight training exercises;
- step-by-step directions to select your exercises and determine how much weight to lift; and
- 75 weight training programs arranged in six progressive workout levels that are geared for three different exercise goals.

For those who are already weight training, this book offers you guidelines for how to effectively cross-train with other types of exercise (like walking, running, biking, or swimming), upgrade your current program (or one found in this book) to improve your performance in a certain sport or activity, and the ultimate task of designing your own program (from scratch).

Acknowledgments

This second edition of *Fitness Weight Training* was completed in the middle of other not-so-small projects, so we are appreciative of the effective assistance and direction provided by several individuals at Human Kinetics. First, to Ed McNeely, Acquisitions Editor, who good-naturedly prodded us along for a few years before passing the baton to Leigh Keylock, Developmental Editor. Thanks, Leigh, for unknowingly volunteering for a photo shoot for another of our textbooks two years prior so we could easily connect a face with a name and a (good) personality when you took over! You were a patient guide in the final eight months and we were pleased to see your type-A attention to detail.

We also appreciate the obvious expertise of Dan Wendt, the Trade Photo Manager, and Joyce Black, the Visual Production Assistant, who made the photo shoot so easy that we were almost worried. Thankfully, the photo shoot models Nicole McBean, Chad Hettmansberger, Mark Gillis, and Susi Huls were cooperative and enthusiastic.

Further, we want to recognize the work done by Robert Replinger, who copyedited this edition so well that it matches the flavor of the first edition while seamlessly including all of the new enhancements. Finally, thanks go to Theresa Campbell, Marketing Manager, Jennifer Altstadt, Marketing Copy Manager, and Cheryl Steiner, Marketing and Publicity Associate, who effectively represented us and the audience of the book; to Nancy Rasmus, who converted the fitness spectrum series version of the first edition to a book with its own unique design; and to Kim Thoren, Assistant Editor, and Tara Welsch, Graphic Artist, who handled the details of layout and proofing. Again, thank you to everyone!

Preparing to Weight Train

Weight training is taking fitness enthusiasts by storm, and it has even become attractive to thousands who once called themselves couch potatoes. Weight training is activity that you can accomplish in a short period, yet it can make dramatic changes in how your body looks and feels. Many who weight train will tell you that having a firm body not only feels great but also positively affects how they relate to others. Weight training can increase your energy level and improve your productivity at work and in many everyday activities.

Weight training helps maintain muscle strength, muscular endurance, neuromuscular (nerve-muscle) coordination, and bone density (helping to prevent osteoporosis). The latest research suggests that weight training contributes significantly to quality of life, whatever one's gender or age. In fact, interest in weight training has increased considerably among seniors and children.

No matter what your weight training experience, you'll find helpful information in this book. If you have little or no experience in weight training, we'll provide the basics to get you started. If you've trained before but without much organization to your approach, you'll benefit from the guidance offered by the structured programs. If you have a great deal of weight training experience, we'll show you how to train better and get more from your workouts. Finally, if you want to weight train to improve performance in your favorite sport, this book will describe how to develop a specific program that focuses on that outcome.

This part of the book begins by describing three different types of training outcomes, which form the basis of the workouts in part II. The remaining chapters in part I lay the groundwork for your weight training program by helping you to

- understand how the physical benefits of weight training compare with other activities;
- determine what weight training equipment to use, where to train, and how to choose and buy equipment;
- assess your weight training fitness;
- choose your desired weight training goal;
- weight train safely and effectively; and
- set up your actual weight training program.

After you have identified your training goal and the appropriate workout level, you will probably be eager to begin your new weight training program. Before jumping in to your first workout, however, be sure that you carefully consider all the guidelines, recommendations, and safety issues explained in this part of the book. Doing so will not only increase the probability of reaching your exercise goals but also reduce your risk of injury.

Let's get started!

1

Weight Train for Fitness

When asked to write the first edition of this book, we said, "Another weight training book? Forget it! There are hundreds already available." We were pleased that we went ahead with the book, however, because the response to our no-nonsense approach was well received. In a matter of months, thousands bought the book and began working out. Our unique method of organizing and presenting workouts enables readers such as you to begin weight training immediately, regardless of current fitness level and experience. After identifying your training goals and training status, you are directed to a specific workout. Easy-to-understand workouts are provided for those who have never trained before as well as for those who have been training for years because the workouts are designed to match your specific fitness level and interest.

No matter what your weight training appetite or fitness level, you'll find something here to satisfy you. The workouts range from easy, short ones for the beginner to intense, lengthier sessions for the highly trained. Best of all, *Fitness Weight Training* is designed to match your individual goals to one of three different outcomes—muscle toning (to tone up muscles), body shaping (to develop larger muscles or shape your body), and strength training (to improve your strength)—and then give you a program to create that outcome and reach your goal.

Muscle Toning

Toned muscles exhibit a tight or firm appearance, rather than a loose or flabby one. They are also defined, which means that you can see distinct muscle separations, indentations, and shapes.

Muscle toning is a natural outcome of regular weight training. If you are interested in muscle toning, higher repetitions in your training will produce better muscle tone qualities without large increases in muscle size. Therefore, the result of following a muscle-toning program will be firmer, harder, and more defined muscles without significant muscle size increases.

Body Shaping

Body-shaping programs provide all the benefits associated with muscle-toning programs, but they also increase the size of muscles more dramatically. With body shaping you'll not only experience the muscle firming and definition of muscle toning but also increase your muscle size. This result is especially true for men; the physique of a woman who is weight training does not change as dramatically. Some women, however, may notice small girth changes in their shoulders, thighs, arms, or back from a body-shaping program.

Strength Training

Strength is the ability of the muscle to exert force. Typically, the term *strength* is associated with the ability to exert maximum force during a single effort, sometimes referred to as a one-repetition maximum effort (1RM). For instance, let's say that you loaded a bar to 100 pounds (45 kg) and were told to perform as many repetitions as possible. If you could do only one repetition, your one-repetition maximum, or 1RM, would equal 100 pounds. Strength increases can contribute significantly to recreational and competitive sport performance as well as make everyday tasks—regardless of your age—a lot easier. Strength-training programs usually produce muscle size gains greater than those produced by toning programs but not to the extent that a body-shaping program will.

Why Not Walk or Jog Instead?

Aerobic exercises such as walking and jogging are ideal for improving the fitness of your heart and lungs and the muscular endurance of your legs, but these activities contribute little to shaping your body and improving your overall flexibility, muscular endurance, and upper-body strength. The advantage of aerobic activities over weight training is that they require minimal equipment and can be done almost anywhere. Swimming, cycling, and cross-country skiing, which are also aerobic activities, contribute better than walking or jogging do to overall flexibility, muscular endurance, and strength, but they still fall short of what weight training programs do for strengthening and shaping specific areas of the body. Weight training programs improve muscular strength, endurance, body composition (ratio of muscle and fat to total body weight), flexibility, and to a much lesser extent, cardiovascular fitness. So, if your goal is to improve cardiovascular fitness, you should include one or more of the aerobic types of exercise mentioned in your training program. But if your goal is to improve your overall flexibility, muscular endurance, strength, and body composition, then you picked the right type of exercise and the right book!

Unlike other exercise activities that rely on developing specific muscles (for example, walking and cycling primarily develop the legs), weight training programs can be designed to develop the legs as well as many other muscle groups—especially those that are particularly important to you. Weight training is like going through a cafeteria and picking which foods you want to eat, instead of having to eat simply what is served to you. The workouts presented in chapters 7 through 9 of this book emphasize exercises for seven major muscle groups (chest, back, shoulders, arms—front and back, abdomen, and legs), but they also affect the muscles of the forearm, calf, and neck. See figures 1.1 and 1.2 on pages 6 and 7 to identify the names and locations of the muscles of the body.

How well your program is designed and how diligently you follow it will determine how successful you are at achieving your desired outcome. What makes weight training exciting is the rapid rate at which you can see and feel changes in your body! As soon as you start exercising, your muscles feel firmer and the "body sculpting" process begins. Regular training will convince you that you have the ability to develop your body in attractive ways that you may never have expected!

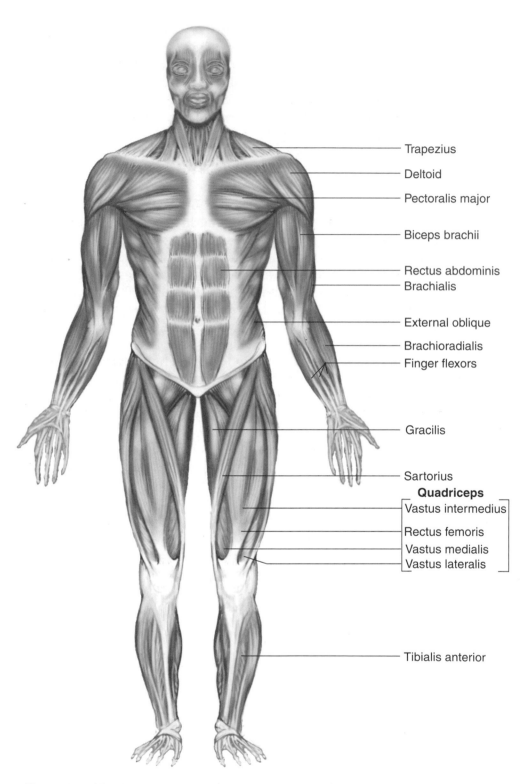

Figure 1.1 Muscles, front view.

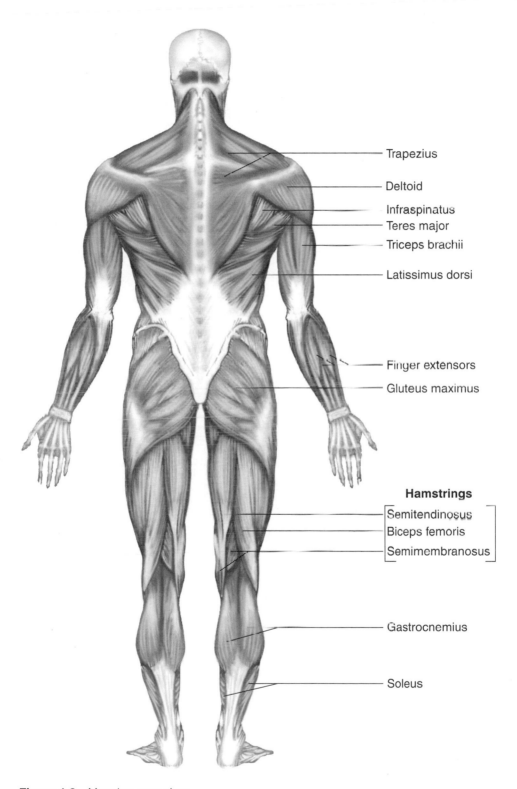

Trapezius

Deltoid

Infraspinatus

Teres major

Triceps brachii

Latissimus dorsi

Finger extensors

Gluteus maximus

Hamstrings

Semitendinosus

Biceps femoris

Semimembranosus

Gastrocnemius

Soleus

Figure 1.2   Muscles, rear view.

## CHAPTER 2

Know Your Equipment

What equipment to use, what to wear, and how to identify a suitable place to train and qualified people to teach you are important considerations for weight training. This chapter will inform you in all these areas so that you can get equipped with confidence! Keep in mind, though, that various types of weight training equipment (especially machines) may have a similar look but feel completely different when you use them.

Types of Weight Training Equipment

Nearly all weight training exercises involve using either a machine or free weights. Both types are found in schools, colleges, health clubs, and corporate settings. For a home facility, machines are typically not a common equipment choice because they require more room (although collapsible machines that save space are becoming more available).

An alternative to a machine or free-weight exercise is one that uses a rubber tube or elastic cable to create resistance. For example, instead of lifting a bar to perform the biceps curl (see page 148), you can use a resistance band (see page 152).

Machines

Machine exercises require you to sit on, lie down in, or stand next to the apparatus. You then move a part of the machine to lift a weight (rather than the weight itself). The two most common types of weight training machines are pivot machines (single- and multiunit) and cam machines.

Pivot Machines (PM)

Pivot machines have one or more stacks of weights that you lift by pulling or pushing a weight arm attached to a pivot point. Single-unit machines are designed to perform one exercise for a certain body area, whereas multiunit machines have various stations that let you work many muscle areas by moving from station to station. An example of a single-unit machine is shown in figure 2.1. Pivot machines have both fixed-pivot and moving-pivot designs, and many multiunit machines use both.

Fixed-resistance pivot machines have one or more fixed weight stacks that you lift by pulling or pushing a weight arm attached to a fixed pivot point. The limitation of this type of equipment is that at some points during the exercise the load does not tax the muscles as much as it does at other points. As a result, different positions require more effort than others do, as though someone were changing the weight during each repetition.

Like the fixed-resistance machine, the variable-resistance pivot machine also has a weight arm attached to a pivot point. But the weight stack moves or rolls back and forth on a weight arm, producing a more consistent load on muscles. When the weight arm moves to a position that would require less effort, the weight stack slides to a position requiring more effort. Conversely, when the weight arm moves to a position that would require more effort, the weight stack moves to a position requiring less effort.

Figure 2.1 A single-unit pivot machine.

Cam Machines (CM)

A cam machine is a variable-resistance machine that features an elliptically shaped wheel, referred to as a cam. The shape of the cam allows a cam machine to function similarly to a variable-resistance pivot machine. As the chain (cable or belt) tracks over the peaks and valleys of the cam, the distance between the point of rotation (the axle on which the cam rotates) and the weight stack varies to produce a more consistent load on the muscles. An example of a cam machine is shown in figure 2.2.

Figure 2.2 A cam machine.

Safety Considerations for Machines

Many consider weight training machines safer than free-weight equipment because the weight stack is positioned and contained so that it cannot fall off or fall on the exerciser. In addition, machine exercises typically do not require the same degree of muscular coordination required by free-weight exercises. Another advantage is that you can perform machine exercises without a spotter. With that said, do not think for a minute that you cannot be seriously injured on a machine. More machine-related injuries than free-weight-related injuries are probably reported each year. By developing an understanding of how to use machines properly (as discussed in chapter 6), you will find them to be a safe and time-efficient type of weight training equipment.

Free Weights

A free-weight exercise allows more freedom to move the weight in nearly any desired direction because you are actually holding the bar, dumbbell, or weight plate. Free weights usually cost less than weight machines and offer tremendous versatility, making your choice of exercises virtually unlimited.

Barbells

Most two-arm and two-leg exercises involve a barbell. The typical barbell has a middle section that includes both smooth and knurled (roughened) areas with collars on each side. The weight plates slide up to collars that stop the plates from sliding inward toward the hands. The outside collars, sometimes referred to as locks, slide up and tighten next to the plates and keep them from sliding off the ends of the bar. A 6-foot (183 cm) bar with collars and locks weighs approximately 30 pounds (14 kg), or 5 pounds per foot (7.6 kg per m) of the bar. Cambered or curl bars have the same characteristics as standard bars except that the curves enable you to isolate certain muscle groups better than you can when using a straight bar.

At weight training and fitness facilities you will usually find 6-foot (183 cm) standard and cambered bars and 7-foot (213 cm) Olympic bars. Olympic bars have the same diameter as most bars except that the diameter is greater in the section between the collar and the end of the bar. Olympic bars are heavier than their standard counterparts are, weighing 45 pounds (20 kg) without locks. Olympic weight plates, which have larger holes than standard weight plates, are designed for use only with Olympic bars. Free-weight equipment is shown in figure 2.3.

Safety Considerations for Free Weights

The term *free* in free weight means that the equipment does not restrict joint movement. Consequently, using free-weight barbells and dumbbells requires a higher level of muscle coordination than using machines. Because of this freedom of movement, injuries are more likely to occur when the exerciser does not use correct loading, lifting, and spotting techniques. When reasonable precautions are taken (as discussed in chapter 6), free-weight training is safe, and it can be more fun than training with machines while also being more effective in strengthening joint structures.

Dumbbells

Dumbbells are used in one- and two-arm exercises. Although they are sometimes premolded (all one piece, without weight plates), training facilities more commonly have dumbbells of a design similar to barbells. Dumbbells are shorter than barbells, and their entire middle section (between weight plates) is usually knurled. A dumbbell bar with collars and locks weighs

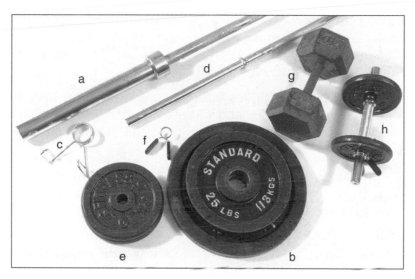

Figure 2.3 Free-weight equipment: *(a)* Olympic bar, *(b)* Olympic-style weight plate, *(c)* Olympic bar lock, *(d)* standard bar, *(e)* standard weight plate, *(f)* standard lock, *(g)* standard dumbbell, *(h)* plate-loaded dumbbell.

approximately 3 pounds (1.4 kg). Usually only the weight of the plates is considered when the weight of the dumbbell is marked on the side of the outermost plate. For example, a dumbbell with a 10-pound plate on both sides is indicated as weighing 20, not 23, pounds.

Resistance Bands

Exercising with resistance bands is a convenient and practical choice if you cannot go to a fitness facility, have limited space at home, or travel frequently. Resistance bands come in various lengths, handle types, and colors (which usually indicate degrees of elasticity).

Safety Considerations for Resistance Bands

Beware of old, worn, or cracked bands that may break at the worst moment when you are using them. Also, check that the handles are securely attached to the rest of the band before you perform an exercise. If you are using a doorknob or piece of furniture as an anchor point, be sure that no one will open the door and that the band is firmly fixed.

Weight Training Attire

Weight training requires no standardized outfit or clothing. You will see everything from tight-fitting, one-piece suits (similar to those worn by wrestlers) to baggy pants and shirts. Men often wear tank tops or T-shirts, shorts, and gym shoes. Women may wear similar clothing or choose to wear shorts over a bodysuit or shorts and a Lycra sports bra (with or without a tank top). Beyond the clothes on your back, you should consider other things to wear while working out.

Gloves. Weight training gloves are not a necessity, but they will help you avoid developing calluses and will provide a better grip. Buy flexible gloves with a leather palm and a mesh back that fit your hands snugly.

Shoes. Wear shoes that have firm support, especially side to side. Look for shoes that have a normal-sized heel width, such as tennis shoes, rather than the wide or waffle heel of running shoes. Cross-training shoes are an excellent choice because they provide the best overall stability and versatility.

Weight belts. Another type of gear seen in weight rooms is a belt 4 to 6 inches (10 to 15 cm) wide made of leather or nylon. Weight belts add support to the lower back, especially during overhead lifting or heavy squatting exercises. Go to chapter 6 for more information about this popular piece of weight training attire.

What not to wear. Before you enter the weight room, take care to remove any items that may cause injury. Earrings, necklaces, watches, and rings can catch on equipment and be ripped off, be smashed, or create abrasions and cuts. Also, if you have long hair, consider pulling it back so that it will not be caught in the moving parts of a machine. The same recommendation and rationale applies to an oversize shirt, sweatshirt, or sweatpants.

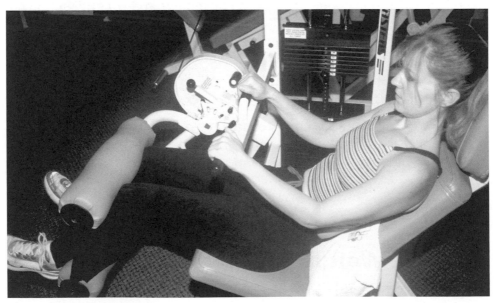

Wearing form-fitting clothing and no jewelry when weight training helps prevent injury.

Weight Training Facilities

You can weight train in one of two places: in your home or at a fitness facility. The following section discusses the pros and cons of each option.

Training at Home

For many, training at home is the only practical option because of time constraints, cost of a fitness facility membership, or both. Many people simply prefer to train in the quiet of their own homes. If you want to train at home, there are several basic equipment and space issues to consider.

Room Location and Design

When selecting a place to train at home, begin by determining a suitable area for storing equipment as well as working out. The location should be out of the way of the main travel routes in your home; it should be well ventilated, well lighted, and have at least one electrical outlet; and it should be securable (if you have young children). An electrical outlet offers the opportunity to plug in a stereo, radio, or maybe a treadmill or stair-stepping machine. If you have a choice, select an area that has a high ceiling.

The floor of a home facility is commonly carpet-covered concrete. Such a surface is better than tile or uncovered concrete because both can be slippery and easily damaged from dropping barbells and dumbbells or moving equipment. Also, arrange the tallest pieces of equipment next to the walls, but allow at least a 6-inch (15 cm) space. If you have more than one machine or bench, give yourself at least 18 inches (46 cm) between them for easy access.

Basic Equipment Requirements

The minimum amount and type of equipment you need to use when following a basic weight program consists of a standard barbell with collars and locks, a set of adjustable dumbbells, 80 pounds (36 kg) of standard weight plates, and a bench with upright racks long enough so that you can lie down with both your head and buttocks squarely on the pad. If you are well trained—or plan to be in the future—you may need to buy an additional 135 pounds (61 kg) of standard weight plates.

For more serious lifters, basic equipment needs include an Olympic bar and locks, a set of dumbbells (in 5-pound increments, possibly up to 50 pounds or more), 255 pounds (116 kg) of Olympic weight plates, and a bench with upright racks to hold an Olympic bar. You may also want to buy a squat rack so that you do not have to pick up the barbell from the floor to do squats or standing shoulder presses. Last, to hold all the weight plates, consider buying a weight tree so that the plates are not in piles on the floor.

Training at a Fitness Facility

Selecting a fitness facility that will meet your needs is a challenge. If you need the expertise of a qualified personal trainer to help you get started, that should be the number-one criterion when selecting where you will work out. Ideally, the facility you choose will have both qualified personnel and a variety of equipment and programs to meet your training needs.

Training With a Personal Trainer

A well-qualified personal trainer who understands how to motivate you can make every training day an enjoyable and rewarding experience. A truly qualified personal trainer will probably have earned one or more certifications associated with the health and fitness profession. Look for someone who has received certification from the National Strength and Conditioning Association (NSCA) as a Certified Strength and Conditioning Specialist or NSCA-Certified Personal Trainer or certification from some other respected fitness-related professional organizations.

Be sure that you obtain a referral from people you trust—or at least observe the personal trainer in action before making a decision. How well a personal trainer is able to make technical information understandable is essential to your success. A good personal trainer will help you understand what you are doing and why you are doing it. In addition, it never hurts to work with someone who has a motivating personality that will energize you to stick to your training program.

Training Without a Personal Trainer

If you are new to weight training and decide to train on your own in a fitness facility, one of your first decisions concerns whether to use weight machines or free weights. Although free weights offer you the tremendous versatility of choosing among many possible exercises, they require more skill. Although machines are not foolproof, they are generally easier and safer, once you learn how to use them properly. Take special care when selecting loads, because sometimes even the lightest weight plate or bar may exceed your strength in a particular exercise. Also, keep in mind that the dimensions of some machines may not accommodate your physique, especially if you are short, tall, or very heavy. For those reasons, it is wise to receive instruction from a qualified professional for at least the first couple of weeks, because he or she can teach you how to perform the exercise and how to make necessary machine adjustments. If you decide to use free weights, obtaining professional instruction is even more important.

## CHAPTER 3

Check Your Weight Training Fitness

Once you decide to begin an exercise program, it is natural to want to do too much too soon. If you're out of shape, remember that you did not get that way in a couple of days. You cannot get back into shape in a couple of days either, so don't try! Your attempts to do so might lead to excessive muscle soreness, extreme fatigue, reduced enthusiasm about resuming training, and possible injury. Use the following Physical Activity Readiness checklist to determine whether you should consult with a physician before you begin working out.

Test Your Weight Training Fitness

Knowing your fitness status will enable you to select a training level that matches your current abilities and will help you establish reasonable goals. Determine your current fitness level for weight training by using the following bench press test. The results of this test will give you a general idea of your readiness to begin weight training. Refer to page 162 in chapter 10 for an illustration of how to perform the free-weight bench press exercise.

Physical Activity Readiness
Questionnaire - PAR-Q
(revised 2002)

PAR-Q & YOU

(A Questionnaire for People Aged 15 to 69)

Regular physical activity is fun and healthy, and increasingly more people are starting to become more active every day. Being more active is very safe for most people. However, some people should check with their doctor before they start becoming much more physically active.

If you are planning to become much more physically active than you are now, start by answering the seven questions in the box below. If you are between the ages of 15 and 69, the PAR-Q will tell you if you should check with your doctor before you start. If you are over 69 years of age, and you are not used to being very active, check with your doctor.

Common sense is your best guide when you answer these questions. Please read the questions carefully and answer each one honestly: check YES or NO.

YES	NO		
☐	☐	1.	**Has your doctor ever said that you have a heart condition <u>and</u> that you should only do physical activity recommended by a doctor?**
☐	☐	2.	**Do you feel pain in your chest when you do physical activity?**
☐	☐	3.	**In the past month, have you had chest pain when you were not doing physical activity?**
☐	☐	4.	**Do you lose your balance because of dizziness or do you ever lose consciousness?**
☐	☐	5.	**Do you have a bone or joint problem (for example, back, knee or hip) that could be made worse by a change in your physical activity?**
☐	☐	6.	**Is your doctor currently prescribing drugs (for example, water pills) for your blood pressure or heart condition?**
☐	☐	7.	**Do you know of <u>any other reason</u> why you should not do physical activity?**

If

you

answered

YES to one or more questions

Talk with your doctor by phone or in person BEFORE you start becoming much more physically active or BEFORE you have a fitness appraisal. Tell your doctor about the PAR-Q and which questions you answered YES.

- You may be able to do any activity you want — as long as you start slowly and build up gradually. Or, you may need to restrict your activities to those which are safe for you. Talk with your doctor about the kinds of activities you wish to participate in and follow his/her advice.
- Find out which community programs are safe and helpful for you.

NO to all questions

If you answered NO honestly to <u>all</u> PAR-Q questions, you can be reasonably sure that you can:
- start becoming much more physically active — begin slowly and build up gradually. This is the safest and easiest way to go.
- take part in a fitness appraisal — this is an excellent way to determine your basic fitness so that you can plan the best way for you to live actively. It is also highly recommended that you have your blood pressure evaluated. If your reading is over 144/94, talk with your doctor before you start becoming much more physically active.

→ **DELAY BECOMING MUCH MORE ACTIVE:**
- if you are not feeling well because of a temporary illness such as a cold or a fever — wait until you feel better; or
- if you are or may be pregnant — talk to your doctor before you start becoming more active.

PLEASE NOTE: If your health changes so that you then answer YES to any of the above questions, tell your fitness or health professional. Ask whether you should change your physical activity plan.

<u>Informed Use of the PAR-Q</u>: The Canadian Society for Exercise Physiology, Health Canada, and their agents assume no liability for persons who undertake physical activity, and if in doubt after completing this questionnaire, consult your doctor prior to physical activity.

No changes permitted. You are encouraged to photocopy the PAR-Q but only if you use the entire form.

NOTE: If the PAR-Q is being given to a person before he or she participates in a physical activity program or a fitness appraisal, this section may be used for legal or administrative purposes.

"I have read, understood and completed this questionnaire. Any questions I had were answered to my full satisfaction."

NAME _____

SIGNATURE _____   DATE _____

SIGNATURE OF PARENT _____   WITNESS _____
or GUARDIAN (for participants under the age of majority)

Note: This physical activity clearance is valid for a maximum of 12 months from the date it is completed and becomes invalid if your condition changes so that you would answer YES to any of the seven questions.

CSEP
SCPE   © Canadian Society for Exercise Physiology   Supported by: [🍁] Health Santé
                                                                         Canada Canada

continued on other side...

Source: Physical Activity Readiness Questionnaire (PAR-Q) © 2002. Reprinted with permission from the Canadian Society for Exercise Physiology. http//www.csep.ca/forms.asp.

PAR-Q & YOU

Physical Activity Readiness
Questionnaire - PAR-Q
(revised 2002)

Get Active Your Way, Every Day—For Life!

Scientists say accumulate 60 minutes of physical activity every day to stay healthy or improve your health. As you progress to moderate activities you can cut down to 30 minutes, 4 days a week. Add-up your activities in periods of at least 10 minutes each. Start slowly... and build up.

Time needed depends on effort

Very Light Effort	Light Effort 60 minutes	Moderate Effort 30-60 minutes	Vigorous Effort 20-30 minutes	Maximum Effort
• Strolling • Dusting	• Light walking • Volleyball • Easy gardening • Stretching	• Brisk walking • Biking • Raking leaves • Swimming • Dancing • Water aerobics	• Aerobics • Jogging • Hockey • Basketball • Fast swimming • Fast dancing	• Sprinting • Racing

Range needed to stay healthy

You Can Do It – Getting started is easier than you think

Physical activity doesn't have to be very hard. Build physical activities into your daily routine.

- Walk whenever you can – get off the bus early, use the stairs instead of the elevator.
- Reduce inactivity for long periods, like watching TV.
- Get up from the couch and stretch and bend for a few minutes every hour.
- Play actively with your kids.
- Choose to walk, wheel or cycle for short trips.

- Start with a 10 minute walk – gradually increase the time.
- Find out about walking and cycling paths nearby and use them.
- Observe a physical activity class to see if you want to try it.
- Try one class to start – you don't have to make a long-term commitment.
- Do the activities you are doing now, more often.

Benefits of regular activity	Health risks of inactivity
• better health • improved fitness • better posture and balance • better self-esteem • weight control • stronger muscles and bones • feeling more energetic • relaxation and reduced stress • continued independent living in later life	• premature death • heart disease • obesity • high blood pressure • adult-onset diabetes • osteoporosis • stroke • depression • colon cancer

Source: Canada's Physical Activity Guide to Healthy Active Living, Health Canada, 1998 http://www.hc-sc.gc.ca/hppb/paguide/pdf/guideEng.pdf

© Reproduced with permission from the Minister of Public Works and Government Services Canada, 2002.

FITNESS AND HEALTH PROFESSIONALS MAY BE INTERESTED IN THE INFORMATION BELOW:

The following companion forms are available for doctors' use by contacting the Canadian Society for Exercise Physiology (address below):

The **Physical Activity Readiness Medical Examination (PARmed-X)** – to be used by doctors with people who answer YES to one or more questions on the PAR-Q.

The **Physical Activity Readiness Medical Examination for Pregnancy (PARmed-X for Pregnancy)** – to be used by doctors with pregnant patients who wish to become more active.

References:
Arraix, G.A., Wigle, D.T., Mao, Y. (1992). Risk Assessment of Physical Activity and Physical Fitness in the Canada Health Survey
Follow-Up Study. **J. Clin. Epidemiol.** 45:4 419-428.
Mottola, M., Wolfe, L.A. (1994). Active Living and Pregnancy, In: A. Quinney, L. Gauvin, T. Wall (eds.), **Toward Active Living: Proceedings of the International
Conference on Physical Activity, Fitness and Health**. Champaign, IL: Human Kinetics.
PAR-Q Validation Report, British Columbia Ministry of Health, 1978.
Thomas, S., Reading, J., Shephard, R.J. (1992). Revision of the Physical Activity Readiness Questionnaire (PAR-Q). **Can. J. Spt. Sci.** 17:4 338-345.

To order multiple printed copies of the PAR-Q, please contact the:

Canadian Society for Exercise Physiology
202-185 Somerset Street West
Ottawa, ON K2P 0J2
Tel. 1-877-651-3755 • FAX (613) 234-3565
Online: www.csep.ca

The original PAR-Q was developed by the British Columbia Ministry of Health. It has been revised by an Expert Advisory Committee of the Canadian Society for Exercise Physiology chaired by Dr. N. Gledhill (2002).

Disponible en français sous le titre «Questionnaire sur l'aptitude à l'activité physique - Q-AAP (revisé 2002)».

 © Canadian Society for Exercise Physiology

Supported by: Health Canada Santé Canada

Bench Press Test

Equipment

- A 35-pound (16 kg) barbell for women or an 80-pound (36 kg) barbell for men
- Flat bench press bench (with upright racks to hold the bar)

Directions

1. Seek the help of a qualified individual to spot (supervise) you as you perform the exercise.
2. Lie on your back with your head, shoulders, upper back, and buttocks on the bench and your feet straddled and flat on the floor.
3. With the palms up, grip the bar at a position slightly wider than shoulder width.
4. With the spotter's assistance, move the bar upward and away from the uprights until your elbows are fully extended and the bar is directly above the nipples.
5. Lower the bar to touch the chest lightly and briefly.
6. Push the bar upward until the elbows are fully extended (but not forcefully locked out); this action completes the first repetition.
7. Continue lowering and pressing the barbell until you cannot complete another repetition with proper technique. Do not pause to rest between repetitions.
8. Record the number of repetitions that you complete.

Be sure to use a spotter when performing the free-weight bench press test.

Important!

Perform each repetition in a slow, controlled manner. Allow one to two seconds to push the bar to the extended-elbow position and one to two seconds to perform the downward movement to the chest. Each repetition should take two to four seconds to complete. Do not bounce the bar off the chest. Remember to breathe out when pushing upward and inhale as you lower the bar, especially when the repetitions become harder to complete.

To determine your score, refer to the top half of table 3.1 if you are male and the lower half if you are female. Identify the appropriate age-range column and below it find the number of repetitions that you completed. At the far left column you'll find your weight training fitness status.

Table 3.1   Muscular Fitness Norms of the Bench Press Test

Weight training fitness status based on the number of completed repetitions

Age	18-25	26-35	36-45	46-55	56-65	≥66
MEN						
Low	≤20	≤17	≤14	≤9	≤5	≤4
Average	21-32	18-28	15-24	10-10	0-13	5-9
High	≥33	≥29	>25	≥20	≥14	≥10
WOMEN						
Low	≤16	≤14	≤12	≤7	≤5	≤5
Average	17-27	15-27	13-23	8-17	6-13	4-9
High	≥28	>28	≥24	≥18	≥14	≥10

Data from J.A. Golding, C.R. Meyers, W.E. Sinning, 1989.

Now that you have determined your fitness status, you are probably eager to begin training, but you should wait until you have read the chapters in this part of the book. Each chapter provides essential information that will enable you to maximize every minute of training. Then, after you've chosen your actual program from those included in part II, go to chapters 6 and 10 to learn how to weight train safely and effectively.

## CHAPTER 4

Make a Successful Start to Your Program

The programs included in this book are organized into six gradually increasing levels. Level 1 workouts are the easiest and take the least time to complete, followed by level 2 through level 5 workouts. The highest level, level 6, contains the most strenuous workouts and takes the most time to complete. Within each of the levels, you'll have an opportunity to select workouts designed to produce muscle-toning, body-shaping, or strength development outcomes. Which workout program should you choose? Your training goal and your current training status determine the answer.

Choose Your Desired Training Goal

Focusing on a specific goal encourages you to make a commitment to training, which in turn motivates you to work out harder and more consistently. To set an effective goal, you need to take a few minutes to consider how you want your body to change because of your weight training program. (You may want to review chapter 1 for a more detailed explanation of the terms *muscle toning, body shaping,* and *strength training* and how they relate to your weight training goals.) Here are some questions to help you focus in on your primary training goal:

- Are you seeking to tone and define your muscles without increasing their size significantly? If so, then the muscle-toning workouts are probably best for you.
- Do you want to firm your muscles and increase muscle definition as well as increase size? If losing fat from certain areas while increasing the size of some muscles is your goal, then the body-shaping workouts are the ones to choose.
- Do you seek improvement in strength for occupational, recreational, or everyday tasks or competitive sports activities? If so, follow the strength-training workouts.

Determine Your Initial Training Level

The goal you selected identifies the type of training outcome you want. Now, you need to determine which workout level matches your current weight training fitness status by referring back to your score on the bench press test (see chapter 3).

Now, look at table 4.1. Use both your past weight training experience (be honest!) and the results of the bench press test to select the appropriate workout level. For example, if you are untrained (new to weight training or have done some weight training in the past but not recently) or if your bench press test revealed that you have low fitness status, start with level 1 workouts. If you are trained (or you have been weight training recently) but have low fitness status, start with level 2 workouts.

Remember that the bench press test is only a guideline. If you are older than 35 or younger than 15 and have not been weight training regularly, you should start in level 1 or 2 regardless of how you scored on the bench press test. If you feel that the workouts in your starting level are too difficult, move to an easier one. A prudent approach is to be somewhat conservative, especially if you are untrained.

Table 4.1	Weight Training Fitness Status and Recommended Initial Training Level	
Weight training fitness status (from the bench press test)	Starting level if you are untrained	Starting level if you are trained
Low	1	2
Average	3	4
High	5	6

After you have identified your primary weight training goal and initial training level, fill in the following chart. To fill in the last item, flip ahead in this book to chapters 7 through 9 (based on your training goal) and locate the page number among levels 1 through 6—that will be your first workout!

My Weight Training Program

- My primary training goal *(circle one):*
  Muscle toning
  Body shaping
  Strength training
- Results of my bench press test: ____ repetitions
- My weight training fitness status *(circle one):*
  Low
  Average
  High
- My initial training level *(circle one):*

  Level 1   Level 4

  Level 2   Level 5

  Level 3   Level 6
- My first weight training workout begins on page ____.

Observe the Keys of Effective Training

Now, to do all that you can to make a successful start to your new program, read the guidelines that follow and then go to chapter 5 to set up your program. Although these suggestions seem to be common sense, they can have a dramatic positive effect on how you feel while weight training.

Train regularly. You are virtually guaranteed success if you follow the workouts presented in this book—which means that you will be training on a regular basis. Sporadic training does not produce results! One of the most effective strategies is to work out with a partner. Being accountable to someone will make you train consistently; just find a partner who has a similar personal schedule and make plans to meet at a certain time on specific days.

Increase workout intensity gradually. To allow your muscles to adjust to the stress of weight training, gradually increase the intensity of your training sessions. The six sequential levels of workouts included in this book keep to this principle.

Don't underestimate the importance of nutrition and rest. Remember the "secret" training formula:

Regular training + Balanced meals + Adequate rest = Dramatic improvements

Amazingly, many people give attention to only one or two of these factors! If one is missing, the results of your program will be less than optimal. Although much has been written on the value of nutritional supplements, especially those high in protein, respected nutritionists continue to stress that balanced meals (approximately 12 percent protein, 58 percent carbohydrates, and 30 percent fat) provide our dietary needs, including protein. An excellent source of nutritional information is *Nancy Clark's Sports Nutrition Guidebook*.

Besides nutrition, your body needs rest to rebuild muscles after training as much as it needs training to stimulate improvement. Initially, you need to train two or three times a week. More is not always better. If you train too often, your muscles don't have enough time to receive nutrition and rebuild, and you may even injure yourself. Training smart means that you train regularly, eat balanced meals, and get enough rest. Taking this approach is critical.

Develop and maintain a positive attitude. Nothing worthwhile comes easy. You have to believe that weight training can produce dramatic improvements in your appearance, fitness, and physical performance—and it does. Get psyched, because you are in for a treat. Every minute, every day makes a difference! Admittedly, training is uncomfortable at times, but perseverance pays off. The burn hurts, but that burn is what molds your body, helps reduce body fat, and accentuates muscle tone. Do not miss a training session; one missed session leads to two, two to three, and then what you could have achieved will not happen. Develop the attitude that the hour you put aside for training is the time that you are doing something for yourself. It's your time, so be selfish with it. In the end you will feel better about yourself and be healthier and more productive. Weight training is the one thing that you can do in an hour that will positively affect your appearance, fitness status, health, and physical performance. Your investment in training time will yield rich rewards!

©Sport the Library

Your training will be maximized when you work purposefully toward a specific goal.

5

Set Up Your Program

This chapter walks you through two steps to follow as you prepare to weight train. The result of completing these steps will round out the details necessary to prepare you and your workout sheet. In addition, you will find extra information on potentially the most confusing part of a weight training program: determining the weight you will use for each exercise.

Step 1: Fill in Your Workout Chart

If you observe people who are in great training shape, you will invariably see them recording information on a chart or booklet. This process is an important part of being successful in your training, because it helps you maintain your interest, allows you to see improvement, and helps you establish reasonable goals. To fill in your workout chart, follow the five guidelines presented here.

1. Locate the workouts. After determining the level at which you plan to start, locate the workout in that level for your desired training outcome. Refer to page 25 where you noted the page number of your first weight-training workout. Note that some are two-day-a-week programs and others are three- and four-day-a-week programs.

2. Make copies of the workout chart. At the top of the page of the workout you selected, you will see the number of days (per week) that you will weight train. Find the correct workout chart in appendix A according to whether you'll train two, three, or four days each week.

Photocopy the workout chart that matches the number of days listed for the workout level. Each chart covers a one-week period of training, and each workout level covers a six-week period, so you will need to make at least six copies of each chart. If you plan to follow the workout longer than six weeks, make an appropriate number of copies of this chart. As you progress from one level to another, follow the same procedure.

3. Choose your training days. You should not weight train the same muscles on two consecutive days or, on the other hand, allow more than three days to go by between workouts. In either case you would be compromising your improvements. So, for example, a two-days-per-week program might follow a Monday and Thursday, Tuesday and Friday, or Wednesday and Saturday schedule. A program that involves three non-consecutive training sessions might follow a Monday, Wednesday, and Friday or Tuesday, Thursday, and Saturday regime.

To determine the most effective way to complete four training sessions per week, choose one of the three options shown in table 5.1. Choose an option that you can adhere to consistently and one that is convenient for you. Each option provides two workouts each for your upper and lower body and spreads out all the workouts so that you have sufficient rest days between similar weight training sessions.

4. Select and record exercises. After considering the equipment available to you and your familiarity with its use, decide which type you will use and record the exercise names onto the workout chart. Notice that each workout level includes exercises for free weights and two types of machines (from which to select single- and multiunit pivot and cam machines). If you are inexperienced, you should begin with machine exercises. Free-weight exercises require more skill than machine exercises do and sometimes require a spotter. In each workout, notice that to the

Table 5.1 Options for a Four-Days-Per-Week Weight Training Schedule

Schedule (days of the week)	Upper-body workouts	Lower-body workouts
Option 1	Mondays and Thursdays	Tuesdays and Fridays
Option 2	Sundays and Wednesdays	Mondays and Thursdays
Option 3	Tuesdays and Fridays	Wednesdays and Saturdays

left of each exercise is the muscle group that is worked by that exercise. Knowing the muscle group enables you to select an alternative exercise to replace one that you may not be able to perform because the equipment needed is not available. Record the exercises that you will perform in the "Exercises" column of the workout chart. If you are not familiar with the exercises listed, refer to chapter 10.

5. Record sets and repetitions.   Refer to the set and repetition information included in the selected workout and transfer those numbers onto the workout chart in the "Sets/Reps" column. Be sure to record the correct set and repetition information for each exercise.

Your workout chart provides a diary of each training day. Be sure to record all the information requested so that you'll be able to recognize the successes that occur as you train on regular basis.

Step 2: Determine Training Loads

Determining a load or weight that you can lift for the required number of repetitions listed in the level workouts is a challenge. What follows is a description of two methods to help you accomplish this task. If you are new to weight training and have no experience in selecting training loads, use the "Level 1 Load Guidelines." If you are experienced, use the "Level 2 Through 6 Load Guidelines."

It's important to carefully determine the correct weight to lift by either calculating a trial load or performing the 1RM test.

Level 1 Load Guidelines

Tables 5.2 and 5.3 are load calculation tables that will help you establish appropriate training loads for level 1 workouts (table 5.2 for women; table 5.3 for men). Use these steps when establishing loads:

1. Look at the exercise names you recorded on your workout chart and then circle the corresponding coefficients ("Factor") on the table. Notice that men and women use different coefficient values, as reflected in the two tables.

2. Record your body weight in the blank in the far left-hand column (labeled "BWT") next to the coefficient column. Important: Men weighing 175 pounds (79 kg) or more and women weighing 140 pounds (64 kg) or more should record 175 (79 kg) and 140 (64 kg), respectively, for their body weight in the "BWT" column.

3. To determine the trial load, multiply your body weight by the coefficient value. The load is called a trial load because you are trying it out to see whether it will result in the required number of repetitions.

4. Round off the trial load to the nearest 5-pound (or 5 kg if you are using plates in kilograms) increment (by rounding down), or if using machines, select the closest weight stack plate (again, by rounding down).

Table 5.2   Load Calculation Table for Women

Exercise	BWT	Factor	Trial load	Reps completed	Adj.	Training load
CHEST						
Bench press (FW)	_____	× .35 =	_____	_____	_____	_____
Bent-arm fly (CM)	_____	× .27 =	_____	_____	_____	_____
Chest press (PM)	_____	× .27 =	_____	_____	_____	_____
BACK						
Bent-over row (FW)	_____	× .35 =	_____	_____	_____	_____
Seated row (CM)	_____	× .20 =	_____	_____	_____	_____
Pullover exercise (CM)	_____	× .20 =	_____	_____	_____	_____
Seated row (PM)	_____	× .25 =	_____	_____	_____	_____
SHOULDERS						
Standing press (FW)	_____	× .22 =	_____	_____	_____	_____
Seated press (PM)	_____	× .15 =	_____	_____	_____	_____
Shoulder press (CM)	_____	× .25 =	_____	_____	_____	_____

Exercise	BWT	Factor	Trial load	Reps completed	Adj.	Training load
BICEPS						
Biceps curl (FW)	_____	× .23 =	_____	_____	_____	_____
Preacher curl (CM)	_____	× .12 =	_____	_____	_____	_____
Low pulley curl (PM)	_____	× .15 =	_____	_____	_____	_____
TRICEPS						
Triceps extension (FW)	_____	× .12 =	_____	_____	_____	_____
Triceps extension (CM)	_____	× .13 =	_____	_____	_____	_____
Triceps pushdown (PM)	_____	× .19 =	_____	_____	_____	_____
LEGS						
Lunge (FW)	5 pounds each hand					
Dual leg press (CM)	_____	× 1.0 =	_____		_____	
Leg press (PM)	_____	× 1.0 =	_____	_____	_____	_____
ABDOMINALS						
Abdominal crunch (CM)	_____	× .20 =	_____	_____	_____	_____

The calculated trial load is designed to allow 12 to 15 repetitions. FW = free weights; CM = cam machine, PM = pivot machine; BWT = body weight. (Remember to use a maximum body weight of 175 pounds [79 kg] for men and 140 pounds [64 kg] for women.)

Table 5.3   Load Calculation Table for Men

Exercise	BWT	Factor	Trial load	Reps completed	Adj.	Training load
CHEST						
Bench press (FW)	_____	× .60 =	_____	_____	_____	_____
Bent-arm fly (CM)	_____	× .55 =	_____	_____	_____	_____
Chest press (PM)	_____	× .55 =	_____	_____	_____	_____
BACK						
Bent-over row (FW)	_____	× .45 =	_____	_____	_____	_____
Seated row (CM)	_____	× .40 =	_____	_____	_____	_____
Pullover exercise (CM)	_____	× .40 =	_____	_____	_____	_____
Seated row (PM)	_____	× .45 =	_____	_____	_____	_____

(continued)

Table 5.3   *(continued)*

Exercise	BWT	Factor	Trial load	Reps completed	Adj.	Training load
SHOULDERS						
Standing press (FW)	_____	× .38 =	_____	_____	_____	_____
Seated press (PM)	_____	× .35 =	_____	_____	_____	_____
Shoulder press (CM)	_____	× .40 =	_____	_____	_____	_____
BICEPS						
Biceps curl (FW)	_____	× .30 =	_____	_____	_____	_____
Preacher curl (CM)	_____	× .20 =	_____	_____	_____	_____
Low pulley curl (PM)	_____	× .25 =	_____	_____	_____	_____
TRICEPS						
Triceps extension (FW)	_____	× .21 =	_____	_____	_____	_____
Triceps extension (CM)	_____	× .35 =	_____	_____	_____	_____
Triceps pushdown (PM)	_____	× .32 =	_____	_____	_____	_____
LEGS						
Lunge (FW)	10 pounds each hand					
Dual leg press (CM)	_____	× 1.3 =	_____	_____	_____	_____
Leg press (PM)	_____	× 1.3 =	_____	_____	_____	_____
ABDOMINALS						
Abdominal crunch (CM)	_____	× .20 =	_____	_____	_____	_____

The calculated trial load is designed to allow 12 to 15 repetitions. FW = free weights; CM = cam machine; PM = pivot machine; BWT = body weight. (Remember to use a maximum body weight of 175 pounds [79 kg] for men and 140 pounds [64 kg] for women.)

Table 5.4 shows an example of how to use table 5.2 to establish a trial load. In this example, the bench press exercise is being used, and the coefficient associated with it is 0.35 (for women). The woman weighs 120 pounds, and the trial load when rounded off (from 42) is 40 pounds.

Try Out the Trial Load

After warming up, perform as many repetitions as you can with the trial load and record that number in the "Reps completed" column. The trial load may be too heavy or too light for a training load.

Make Load Adjustments (Level 1)

If you were able to perform more than 15 reps or were not able to perform 12 reps, refer to table 5.5 to help you identify the correct training load.

Table 5.4 Example of Calculating the Trial Load

Exercise	BWT	Factor	Trial load	Reps completed	Adj.	Training load
CHEST						
Bench press (FW)	*120*	× .35 =	*40*	___	___	___
Bent-arm fly (CM)	___	× .27 =	___	___	___	___
Chest press (PM)	___	× .27 =	___	___	___	___

Table 5.5 Load Adjustment Table

Repetitions completed	Adjustment (in pounds)
≤7	−15
8-9	−10
10-11	−5
12-15	0
16-17	+5
18-19	+10
≥20	+15

Adapted, by permission, from T.R. Baechle, B.R. Groves, 1998, *Weight training: steps to success*, 2nd ed. (Champaign, IL: Human Kinetics), 43.

Table 5.6 is an example of how to use the load calculation and load adjustment tables to create an appropriate training load. In this example, a man needs to calculate his training load for the bench press. For men, the coefficient associated with this exercise is 0.60. The man's trial load equaled 100 pounds (rounded off), and he performed 9 reps (instead of 12 to 15) with this load. According to the load adjustment table, completing 9 reps requires an adjustment of minus 10 pounds. So, in this example, the man subtracts 10 pounds from the trial load using table 5.5, yielding a training load of 90 pounds; he then records his calculated training load onto the load calculation table to the right of the bench press exercise. Use this procedure with all the exercises included in the workouts listed in any level 1 program.

Table 5.6 Example of Using the Load Adjustment Table

Exercise	BWT	Factor	Trial load	Reps completed	Adj.	Training load
CHEST						
Bench press (FW)	*165*	× .60 =	*100*	*9*	*-10*	*90*
Bent-arm fly (CM)	___	× .55 =	___	___	___	___
Chest press (PM)	___	× .55 =	___	___	___	___

Level 2 Through 6 Load Guidelines

If you choose one of the more advanced workout levels, you should use the one-repetition maximum (1RM) method for determining loads for some of the exercises in your workout. This method is significantly more demanding than using the load guidelines presented for beginners in level 1 in a single all-out effort. This 1RM approach is appropriate only for use with exercises that involve large muscle groups, such as the chest, shoulders, and thighs and hips (referred to as *core* exercises). Attempting a 1RM in a noncore exercise that recruits smaller muscle groups—such as those found in the forearms, arms, neck, or calves—increases your chances for injury, because such muscles and joints may not be able to withstand the physical stress of lifting maximal loads. Table 5.7 lists exercises in this book that you can safely perform using the 1RM approach (as long as you use proper procedures).

Table 5.7	Exercises Suitable for a 1RM Effort	
Muscle group	**Core exercises**	**Exercise type**
Chest	Bench press	*FW, PM
	Chest press	CM
Shoulders	Standing press	*FW
	Seated press	PM
	Shoulder press	CM
Thigh	Squat	*FW
	Angled leg press	*FW
	Leg press	PM
	Horizontal leg press	PM, CM

FW = free weights; PM = pivot machine; CM = cam machine

*All free-weight exercises listed require an experienced spotter.

1RM Procedure for Core Exercises

Essentially, your task involves starting with a light warm-up load and progressively adding weight until, after five or six sets, you arrive at your 1RM. To be safe, you should approach the 1RM with these priorities in mind:

- Perform the exercise with proper technique.
- Select the correct load to lift in each 1RM attempt.
- Use a two- to four-minute rest period between attempts.
- Recruit a qualified person to spot you (if the exercise requires it).

If you have never attempted a 1RM, don't try it without first consulting a qualified strength and conditioning or personal-training professional. Free-weight exercises require a skilled spotter, and all exercises require a reasonable level of previous physical training. Unless you are completely confident in your ability to perform the exercise correctly or have access to a qualified professional who can teach you the proper techniques, do not attempt to perform a 1RM! Table 5.8 summarizes the procedures for assessing a 1RM for core exercises. Carefully follow these directions to identify your 1RM.

Table 5.8   Assessing the 1RM in Core Exercises for Levels 2 Through 6

Set #	Estimate of appropriate load (or amount of weight to add):	. . . you perform this number of reps:	. . . and rest for at least this long:
1	You could perform 20 reps with this load, but . . .	12	2 minutes
2	You could perform 10 reps with this load, but . . .	6	2 minutes
3	You could perform 5 to 6 reps with this load, but . . .	3	2 minutes
4	(add 10 pounds)	1	2 to 4 minutes
5	(add 10 pounds)	1	2 to 4 minutes
*6	(add 10 pounds)	1	

*Continue adding 10 pounds as needed until you can no longer lift the weight. When failure occurs, reduce the load by 5 pounds, rest two or more minutes, and try to perform one repetition. The heaviest weight you successfully lifted is your 1RM for that exercise.

Determine Training Loads for Core Exercises

Testing for your 1RM is the first of two steps for determining a training load for core exercises. The second step involves the use of table 5.9 in conjunction with the workout you plan to follow. Simply locate the "Goal repetitions" column heading, which tells you the number of reps to be performed, and then in the "1RM value" column, locate the poundage found for the 1RM. Where these two columns intersect is the training-load poundage. If needed, round off (down) the weight to the nearest five pounds or, when using machines, the nearest weight stack plate.

For example, imagine that you are following one of the strength-training workouts. The goal reps for an exercise such as the seated press is listed as 6, and your 1RM in this exercise is 170. The 6 to 7 reps column and the 170 1RM value intersect at the number 141. By rounding off to the nearest 5 pounds, you establish a training load of 140 for the seated press. You then enter this value on the workout chart.

Table 5.9 Determining Training Loads for Level 2 Through 6 Workouts

1RM value	GOAL REPETITIONS					
	12-15	10-12	8-9	6-7	4-5	2-3
	TRAINING LOADS					
30	18	21	23	25	26	28
35	21	24	27	29	30	33
40	24	28	31	33	35	37
45	27	31	35	37	39	42
50	30	35	39	42	44	47
55	33	38	42	46	48	51
60	36	42	46	50	52	56
65	39	45	50	54	57	60
70	42	49	54	58	61	65
75	45	52	58	62	65	70
80	48	56	62	66	70	74
85	51	59	65	71	74	79
90	54	63	69	75	78	84
95	57	66	73	79	83	88
100	60	70	77	83	87	93
110	66	77	85	91	96	102
120	72	84	92	100	104	112
130	78	91	100	108	113	121
140	84	98	108	116	122	130
150	90	105	116	125	131	140
160	96	112	123	133	139	149
170	102	119	131	141	148	158
180	108	126	139	149	157	167
190	114	133	146	158	165	177
200	120	140	154	166	174	186
210	126	147	162	174	183	195
220	132	154	169	183	191	205
230	138	161	177	191	200	214
240	144	168	185	199	209	223
250	150	175	193	208	218	233
260	156	182	200	216	226	242
270	162	189	208	224	235	251

1RM value	GOAL REPETITIONS					
	12-15	10-12	8-9	6-7	4-5	2-3
	TRAINING LOADS					
280	168	196	216	232	244	260
300	180	210	231	249	261	279
310	186	217	239	257	270	288
320	192	224	246	266	278	298
330	198	231	254	274	287	307
340	204	238	262	282	296	316
350	210	245	270	291	305	326
360	216	252	277	299	313	335
370	222	259	285	307	322	344
380	228	266	293	315	331	353
390	234	273	300	324	339	363
400	240	280	308	332	348	372

*When possible, you should round the load down to the nearest five-pound (or five-kilogram) increment.

Determine Training Loads for Noncore Exercises

For those exercises listed in your workout that are not core exercises, try to identify a load that will result in the repetitions listed in table 5.10 based on the exercise goal.

Table 5.10 Load Guidelines for Noncore Exercises

Outcome desired	Load selected should result in
Muscle toning	12-15 reps
Body shaping	10-12 reps
Strength training	8-10 reps

Make Load Adjustments (Levels 2 Through 6)

After you have determined loads for the various exercises, you will likely find that they are too heavy or too light and do not result in the desired number of reps. If you find that this happens in one or more exercises, complete the following steps to make proper load adjustments:

1. Determine, locate, and circle the goal reps in the left-hand column of table 5.11.
2. Beneath the heading "Repetitions completed," locate and circle the actual appropriate range.

3. Where the "Goal Reps" row and "Repetitions Completed" column intersect is the load adjustment.

4. To establish a new training load, decrease (–) or increase (+) the poundage listed to the original load.

For example, you want to complete 10 reps ("Goal Reps") with 110 pounds, but you are able to perform 15 reps. As shown, the goal reps of 10 intersects the number 15 at +10 pounds. When you add 10 to the 110-pound load, the adjusted load is 120 pounds. Remember, you may have to make several adjustments to establish an accurate training load.

Table 5.11 Level 2 Through 6 Load Adjustment Table

		REPETITIONS COMPLETED WITH THE TRIAL LOAD									
		≥18	16-17	14-15	12-13	10-11	8-9	6-7	4-5	2-3	<2
	14-15	+10	+5		–5	–10	–15	–15	–20	–25	–30
	12-13	+15	+10	+5		–5	–10	–15	–15	–20	–25
GOAL REPS	**10-11**	+15	+15	+10	+5		–5	–10	–15	–15	–20
	8-9	+20	+15	+15	+10	+5		–5	–10	–15	–15
	6-7	+25	+20	+15	+15	+10	+5		–5	–10	–15
	4-5	+30	+25	+20	+15	+15	+10	+5		–5	–10
	2-3	+35	+30	+25	+20	+15	+15	+10	+5		–5
		LOAD INCREASE (+) OR DECREASE (–)									

## CHAPTER 6

Weight Train the Right Way

Weight training is more than simply finding a barbell and "pumping iron." This chapter outlines some dos and don'ts that will help you train safely and get the most out of the time and effort that you devote to training. You should read this chapter and understand the basics of proper weight training exercise technique before you actually begin doing the exercises. In addition, knowing how to prepare to work out (the warm-up) and how to relax gradually after working out (the cool-down) will go a long way toward making each session successful.

Learn Lifting Fundamentals

Although weight training exercises number in the hundreds, several guidelines are universal: Use a good grip, a stable body position, and effective techniques to pick up and put down bars. You must also make good decisions about weight belt use and breathing during an exercise.

Grip the Bar

Grasping a bar involves two considerations: the type of grip to use and the spacing of the hands on the bar.

The grips that people may use on a bar are the *pronated,* or overhand, grip; the *supinated,* or underhand, grip; and the mixed, or *alternated,* grip (see figure 6.1). In the overhand grip the knuckles face up and the thumbs are toward each other. In the underhand grip, the palms face up and the thumbs face away from each other. In the alternate grip, one hand is in an underhand grip and the other in an overhand grip; the thumbs point in the same direction.

All these grips are termed *closed* grips, meaning that the fingers and thumbs are wrapped (closed) around the bar. In an *open* grip, sometimes referred to as a false grip, the thumbs do not wrap around the bar. The open grip can be dangerous because the bar may roll off the palms of the hand and onto the face or foot, causing severe injury. Always use a closed grip!

Several grip widths are used in weight training. In some exercises, lifters place the hands at about shoulder width, at an equal distance from the weight plates. Some exercises require a narrower grip than this, such as at hip width. Other exercises require a wider grip. Figure 6.2 shows different grip widths. When referring to the exercises later in this chapter, be sure to note the type of grip and the proper width for each exercise as

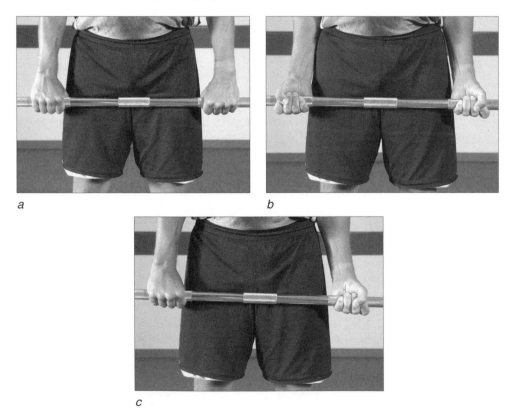

a   b

c

Figure 6.1   Types of grip: *(a)* pronated, or overhand, grip; *(b)* supinated, or underhand, grip; and *(c)* mixed, or alternated, grip.

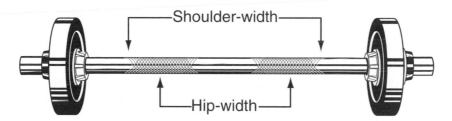

Figure 6.2 Grip widths.

well as how to establish a balanced grip on the bar. Become familiar with the smooth and rough (knurled) areas of the bar and place your hands appropriately. Incorrectly placed hands can create an unbalanced grip and result in serious injury.

Lift the Bar off the Floor

Lifting the bar correctly is important to your safety. Improper lifting places substantial stress on the neck, upper and lower back, and knees—stress that can result in serious injury. Establishing a stable base of support is especially important for overhead exercises with dumbbells or barbells. Furthermore, you need proper mechanics to pick up the bar (or anything, for that matter). Always observe these keys to proper lifting:

- Position your feet flat on the floor, shoulder-width apart with toes pointing ahead or slightly outward.

- Position your shoulders over the bar, keeping your head up and your eyes looking straight ahead.

- Establish the "flat back" position, keeping your back rigid so that when you lift the weight, your legs will do the work.

- As you lift, think, "Keep the bar close, the hips low, and the back flat."

The photo sequence in figure 6.3 on page 42 shows how to lift a barbell safely. The preparatory lifting position (figure 6.3, a and b) places the body in a stable position, one in which the legs—not the back—do the lifting. Getting into the proper position is not as easy as you might think. As you squat down, one or both heels will tend to lift up, causing you to step forward to catch your balance. Remember, keep your heels on the floor! If a mirror is available, watch yourself as you squat down into the low preparatory position. Does your back stay in a flat position? Do your heels stay in contact with the floor? They should. The most important point to remember when you lift a barbell, dumbbell, weight plate, or any object off the floor is to use your leg muscles, not your back muscles.

If you need to pull the barbell to your shoulders, continue pulling it past your knees (figure 6.3c), but do not allow the bar to rest on your thighs. As you straighten your legs, your hips should move forward quickly, and a rapid shoulder shrug should follow. To pull the bar from the thighs to the shoulders effectively and safely, visualize yourself jumping up with the barbell while keeping your elbows straight (figure 6.3d), and at the very peak of the jump, see yourself shrugging your shoulders and flexing your elbows to catch the bar on the shoulders, as shown in figure 6.3e. Try to synchronize the moment when you catch the bar on or at your shoulders with the time when you land back down on the floor from the jumping portion of the exercise.

a   *b*   *c*

d   *e*

Figure 6.3 Proper barbell lifting technique: *(a)* beginning position, *(b)* first pull, *(c)* scoop, *(d)* second pull, *(e)* catch.

Return the Bar to the Floor

When lowering the bar or any heavy object to the floor, remember to keep the bar or weight close to you and to keep your back flat and rigid, relying on your legs to squat down to move the bar in a slow, controlled manner back to the floor. If the bar begins at shoulder height, allow the weight of the bar to pull your arms out and down, an action that will cause the bar to press against your thighs. Hold the bar briefly at midthigh before squatting down to lower the bar further to the floor. Remember to keep your head up and your back flat throughout the return of the bar to the floor.

When to Wear a Weight Belt

Should you wear a weight belt? The answer depends on which exercise you are performing and the amount of weight you are using. Here are two guidelines:

- You don't need a weight belt for exercises that do not place any stress on the lower back. Common exercises that do not require a weight belt are the lat pulldown, bench press, biceps curl, and leg extension. In other words, don't put on a weight belt for your first exercise and wear it for the rest of your workout because most exercises—when performed properly—do not apply specific stress on your lower back. If you "feel something" in that area during an exercise, it is a sign that you are likely doing the exercise incorrectly rather than an indication that you need a weight belt.

- You should definitely wear a belt when performing exercises that stress the back and involve the use of maximum or near-maximum loads. When using a belt, pull it snugly around you and remember that using a weight belt in and of itself will not protect you from back injuries—good technique will!

Breathing Correctly

Correct breathing while weight training can be summed up in two words: breathe naturally. The result is an even rhythm of breathing in and breathing out without holding the breath. More specifically, you should exhale as you pass through the "sticking point," which is the most difficult part of the work phase of the exercise movement. For example, the sticking point of the biceps curl exercise is approximately halfway through the upward arc of the bar; for the bench press exercise, it is where the bar is a few inches off the chest as you try to push it upward. Inhalation, then, should be during the relaxation phase as you move the bar, dumbbell, or machine back to its starting position.

You will have a tendency to hold your breath throughout the entire exertion phase—avoid doing this, because it is dangerous! If you don't exhale, you reduce the return of blood to your heart and brain, which can make you feel dizzy and lightheaded, and may cause you to faint. Holding your breath is especially dangerous when performing overhead exercises, particularly if you have high blood pressure. Put simply, proper breathing is extremely important during weight training.

Train With Care

The following precautions will make training safer and more effective by helping you avoid potentially dangerous situations. Often such directions or warnings are posted on a wall in a fitness facility or on the placard of a machine or exercise station. Although many of these precautions seem sensible, you will often see other people not following them, so be aware of your surroundings, especially during the busy times of a fitness facility before work, during the noon hour, and after work.

Using Free Weights

Although free-weight exercises provide the greatest degree of movement freedom, this advantage can be a liability. An increase in the possibilities of how you can move a bar, dumbbell, or weight plate also means an increase in the number of potentially hazardous circumstances.

Load bars properly.   Take great care to load bars evenly and with the proper weight. If the ends of a suspended bar (where it is resting on the upright supports or rack) are not loaded evenly, the bar may tip, possibly resulting in injury. Learning to recognize the weight of different bars and of weight plates will help you in loading the bar evenly and in placing the proper amount of load on the bar.

Lock barbells and dumbbells.   Lifting with unlocked barbells and dumbbells is dangerous. Weight plates that are not secured with locks can easily slide off the bar and land on your feet or other body parts. Before performing every set of exercises, you should check both locks for tightness. Do not assume that the last person using the barbell or dumbbell tightened the locks.

Avoid backing into others.   Take care to avoid backing into others, because an untimely bump may cause a barbell or dumbbell to fall on your head (from an overhead exercise) or face (from a lying-down or supine exercise), on the head or face of someone training nearby, or both.

Be aware of extended bars.   Extended bars are those that overhang or extend outward from machines (like the lat pulldown exercise; see chapter 10), barbells supported on large racks (like on a squat rack), bench uprights, or bars held in the hands of other people who are working out. Pay special attention to bars that are positioned at or above shoulder height; serious facial injuries can result from walking into them, so be careful!

Store equipment properly.   Each piece of equipment in the weight training area should be stored in a special location. People can trip or slip on barbells, dumbbells, and weight plates that are left unattended or not placed in their proper locations. Make sure that you put your equipment away immediately after using it, both at home and when you are working out in a fitness facility. If you have children at home you may face an added danger if they are able to climb on equipment or try to lift plates and bars that are too heavy for them. Secure weight training equipment so that children do not have access to it without your supervision.

Using Machines

Although the mechanics of lifting on a machine are less complicated, following a few steps will help ensure safe lifting:

- Always select the correct load and insert the T or L shaped selector key all the way in. Do not use any type of key that does not come with the specific machine.

- Adjust the machine to accommodate your body size, and refer to signs or illustrations (if provided) for the location of the adjustment knobs or dials. If placards do not exist or you are not sure how to make adjustments, request help from a qualified person.

- Establish a stable support base when performing exercises that involve positioning your feet on the floor or positioning your head, torso, hips, or legs on or against the equipment.

- Fasten seat belts securely (if provided).

- Perform exercises through the full range of motion and always in a slow and controlled manner.

- Do not allow the weight plates to slam against the rest of the stack during the lowering phase or to hit the pulleys during the raising phase.

If a piece of equipment doesn't work properly, ask for help. Never place your hands or fingers between weight stacks to dislodge a selector key that is stuck, and keep your hands and fingers (and long hair!) away from moving chains, belts, pulleys, and cams.

Warm Up and Cool Down

Preparing the body to weight train is just as important as doing the actual workout. Without a warm-up, you often will not be able to lift as much, and even attempting to lift will not feel comfortable. Following your workout, you need to decrease your activity level gradually to let your body rest and recover.

Warm Up

The warm-up is an essential part of any well-conceived weight training program. Warm-up activities raise the body temperature and increase blood flow to the muscles, making them more pliable and less likely to become injured when challenged to contract against heavy loads. Activities such as walking, jogging, stationary cycling, stair climbing or stair stepping, rowing, and rope skipping are excellent general body warm-up exercises. Another type of warm-up involves performing the exercise that you are warming up for but with a very light load for 8 to 15 repetitions. This specific (versus general) type of warm-up provides the opportunity for you to get your brain and muscles working in harmony before you tax them with heavier loads. This type of warm-up also gives you the chance to acquire a better sense or feel for which muscles are involved and how to get them more involved in the exercise. Once you have completed 10 or 15 minutes of general warm-up, consider performing a set of 8 to 15 repetitions before the first actual set of an exercise. The combination of both types of warm-up will prepare you mentally as well as physically for the training session.

Stretch

You should include stretching activities for each major muscle group and several for the lower back at the end of the warm-up period. Stretching is more successful after the warm-up than before it because muscles are more flexible and more easily stretched when they are warm. Be careful when performing stretching exercises; otherwise, you may injure yourself. Follow these guidelines as you stretch:

- Move slowly into the stretched position and stretch to a point where you can feel tension, not pain.
- Relax, breathe in deeply, and then exhale.
- Hold the stretch for 15 to 30 seconds and then return slowly to the starting position.
- Perform each stretch at least twice.

The following pages describe and show the common techniques for performing basic flexibility exercises.

Chest and Shoulders

Major muscles stretched: pectoralis major and deltoids

With your elbows straight, grasp your hands together behind your back and slowly lift your arms upward. If you are not able to grasp your hands, simply reach back as far as possible. For an additional stretch, bend forward at the waist and raise your arms higher.

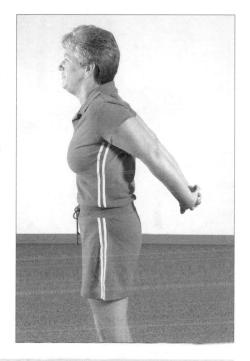

Upper Back, Shoulders, and Back of the Arms

Major muscles stretched: rhomboids, deltoids, and triceps brachii

With your left hand, grasp your right elbow and pull it slowly across your chest toward your left shoulder. Repeat with the other arm.

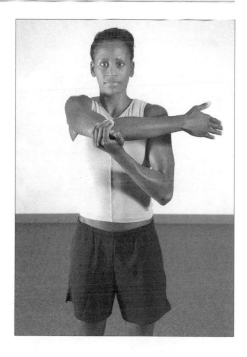

Upper Back and Back of the Arms

Major muscles stretched: latissimus dorsi and triceps brachii

Bring both arms overhead and hold your right elbow with your left hand. Bend your right arm at the elbow and let your right hand touch your upper back. Pull with your left hand to move the right elbow slowly behind your head until you feel a stretch. Repeat with the other arm.

Back and Hips

Major muscles stretched: erector spinae and gluteus maximus

Sit on the floor with your legs straight in front of you. Bend your right leg, cross it over your left knee, and place the sole of your right foot flat on the floor to the outside of your left knee. Next, push against the outside of your upper right thigh with your left elbow, just above the knee. Place your right hand behind you and then slowly rotate your upper body toward your right hand and arm. Repeat with the left leg placed over the right leg and rotate toward your left hand.

Quadriceps

Major muscles stretched: quadriceps

Using a wall or stationary object for balance, grasp your right foot with the right hand and pull so that your heel moves toward your right buttock (the alignment of foot and buttock is important to avoid stress on the knee). You should feel the stretch along the front of your right thigh. Repeat with the other leg.

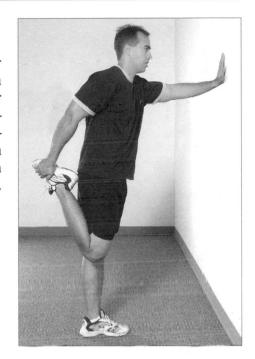

Hamstrings and Lower Back

Major muscles stretched: hamstrings and erector spinae

Sit on the floor with your legs straight out in front of you. Flex your right leg, rotate your right hip to point your right knee out to the side, and place the bottom of your right foot lightly against the inside of your left knee. Slowly

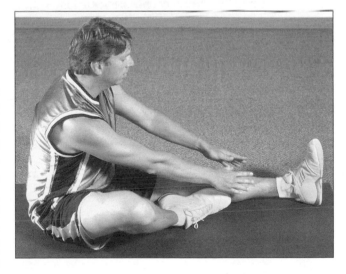

lean forward from your hips to move your torso toward your left knee. Be sure to keep the toes of your left foot pointing up with your ankles and toes relaxed. Switch the position of your legs and repeat with your right leg straight out in front of you.

49

Calves

Major muscles stretched: soleus and gastrocnemius

Stand about 3 feet (91 cm) away from a wall or stationary object. Keeping your right heel in contact with the floor, place your left foot 1 foot (30 cm) in front of your right foot with your left knee slightly flexed. With your right knee straight, lean forward with your entire body without flexing forward at your waist. Keep your right heel on the floor and your back straight Repeat with other leg.

Cool Down

Stopping abruptly when you finish your last set of exercises may cause you to become dizzy, nauseated, or both. Cooling down with a 5- to 10-minute walk, an easy jog, or a series of stretching exercises will provide time to recirculate blood back to the heart from specific muscle groups, an action that will help you avoid feeling ill. Stretching during the cool-down period also provides an ideal opportunity to improve your flexibility, because the muscles and connective tissue surrounding the joints are warm and pliable. An additional benefit of stretching during the cool-down is that it may speed your recovery from muscle soreness.

Training by the Workout Levels

Up to this point, you have learned about the contributions and outcomes of a weight training program, common gear and equipment, your current training status and desired goal, and the steps involved in setting up your program. What's missing? Yes, the actual program itself!

This section includes 76 workout charts that are based on the three goals of weight training: muscle toning (chapter 7), body shaping (chapter 8), and strength training (chapter 9). Within each chapter are six progressively more demanding workout levels (1 through 6).

Understanding the Workout Levels

Each workout chart provides the following information:

- The total time it will take to complete the workout, including warm-up and cool-down periods.
- The number of weeks and the number of times per week that you will complete the workout. For example, for the muscle-toning program, you should perform the level 1, workout 1 for two weeks at a rate of two nonconsecutive training sessions per week.
- A description of the weight training session in detail, including the exercises you are to perform, the number of reps and sets, and the muscle groups worked. The charts have three columns of exercises

(each is a different type; see chapters 5 and 10 for more details), and you will choose one exercise (not all three) for each of the seven major muscle groups: chest, back, shoulders, front of the upper arm (biceps), back of the upper arm (triceps), thighs, and abdomen. Higher workout levels include more exercises that train these muscles as well as others. Note that you are to perform free-weight exercises with a barbell unless the exercise is specifically called a dumbbell exercise. If you have never performed an exercise or are unsure about correct exercise techniques, please review chapter 10 or consult a professional. Remember to use a spotter in all free-weight exercises that require one.

- Guidelines for the duration and type of warm-up and cool-down exercises you should perform.

- A recommendation for how much time you should spend between sets and exercises. During this period, relax by simply sitting or standing at your exercise station, lightly stretching the muscles that you have just exercised, or preparing the bar, dumbbell, or machine for your next set or exercise.

- Workout tips that give more detail about how to complete that specific workout, answer common concerns or questions, or offer suggestions about how to get the most out of your training.

Level 1

The first level is for you if you are new to weight training or if you have not been weight training recently and have low fitness status based on the bench press test. The very low-intensity workouts in this level are structured to initiate you gradually to weight training and to make you feel more confident and comfortable in the weight room.

Level 2

The second level is for you if you have been weight training recently on a consistent basis and have low fitness status based on the bench press test *or* if you completed level 1 and are looking for a more advanced program. The workouts in this level provide a solid base for the more intense levels to follow.

Level 3

The third level is for you if you have not been weight training recently on a consistent basis* and have average fitness status based on the bench press test *or* if you completed level 2 and are looking for a more advanced program. The workouts in this level are more intense, and they help provide a base for the workouts in the advanced levels.

Level 4

The fourth level is for you if you have been weight training recently on a consistent basis and have average fitness status based on the bench press test *or* if you completed level 3 and are looking for a more advanced program. The workouts in this level will help you prepare for more intense workouts of the last two levels.

Level 5

The fifth level is for you if you have not been weight training recently on a consistent basis* and have high fitness status based on the bench press test *or* if you completed level 4 and are looking for a more advanced program. The workouts in this level are intense and require dedication if you want to be successful.

Level 6

The sixth level is for you if you have been weight training recently on a consistent basis and have high fitness status based on the bench press test *or* if you completed level 5 and are looking for a more advanced program. The workouts in this level represent a serious commitment to following an advanced program.

After you have completed the workouts in each level, you have the option to repeat the level, continue to the next level, or design your own personalized program. If you are curious about your progress, you can reassess yourself in the bench press test described in chapter 3. Whatever path you choose, be sure to follow the guidelines in chapter 11 to ensure your continued success. Good luck!

---

* Important: Although an average or high score from the bench press test is good, realize that these levels are challenging to everyone, especially if you have not been weight training recently on a consistent basis. If you feel that the workouts in your starting level are too difficult, move to an easier one.

## CHAPTER 7

Muscle Toning

This type of weight training program is designed to create firmer muscles without causing large changes in size. In addition, you will likely notice that your muscles will have better endurance; you will be able to keep them active for longer periods before becoming tired.

Training Goal Highlights

Level 1

- The muscle-toning program begins with two workouts a week that consist of one set of 12 to 15 reps for seven exercises. The program includes an exercise for each major muscle group: chest, back, shoulders, front of the upper arm (biceps), back of the upper arm (triceps), thighs, and abdomen.
- The number of sets increases from one to two in the third week, and by the fifth week you will be performing those two sets back to back.

Level 2

- The muscle-toning program continues the 12 to 15 reps from level 1 and gradually adds another set (by the fifth week you will be doing three back to back).

Level 3

- A major change in level 3 is that you will be completing three workouts a week instead of two. Because of this increase, weeks 1 and 2 require you to complete only two sets per exercise. Weeks 3 through 6 gradually return you to two to three back-to-back sets.

Level 4

- The first two weeks require three sets of 12 to 15 reps in all seven exercises for three workouts a week.

- Weeks 3 through 6 include three additional exercises—one set of 12 to 15 reps each for your chest, back, and calves. To determine what loads you should use in the new exercises, follow the guidelines in chapter 5.

Level 5

- Weeks 1 and 2 require only two sets in the three additional exercises; by the end of week 4 you will be completing three sets in all 10 exercises. The final two weeks add one set (now you will be doing four) in the seven original exercises.

Level 6

- Weeks 1 and 2 add three more exercises—one set of 12 to 15 reps each for your shoulders and the front and back of your thighs. To determine what loads you should use in the new exercises, refer to chapter 5.

- By the end of week 6 of level 6, you will be performing three to four sets of 12 to 15 repetitions in 13 exercises three times per week!

Level 1   Workout 1

Total time: 44 minutes

Weeks: 1 and 2

Days of the week: Two nonconsecutive days*

Warm-up: Easy jogging or rope skipping for 5 minutes followed by stretching

Exercises: 14 minutes

Number	Muscle group	Reps	Sets	Free weight	Pivot machine	Cam machine
1	Chest	12-15	1	Bench press	Bench press	Chest press
2	Back	12-15	1	One-arm dumbbell row	Lat pulldown	Machine pullover
3	Shoulders	12-15	1	Standing press	Seated press	Shoulder press
4	Front of arm	12-15	1	Biceps curl	Low pulley curl	Preacher curl
5	Back of arm	12-15	1	Dumbbell triceps extension	Triceps pushdown	Triceps extension
6	Thighs	12-15	1	Lunge	Leg press	Horizontal leg press
7	Abdomen	12-15	1	Sit-up	Abdominal crunch	Abdominal crunch

Rest period: 30 seconds**

Cool-down: Slow walking for 5 minutes followed by stretching

Workout tips

* Be sure to spread out your weight training sessions throughout the week; you need at least one rest day (but no more than three) between workouts. A common two-days-per-week program is Monday and Thursday or Wednesday and one weekend day.

** You may want to rest for up to 60 seconds between exercises for your first or second week of training, or both.

Level 1   Workout 2

Total time: 51 minutes

Weeks: 3 and 4

Days of the week: Two nonconsecutive days

Warm-up: Easy jogging or rope skipping for 5 minutes followed by stretching

Exercises: 21 minutes

Number	Muscle group	Reps	Sets*	Free weight	Pivot machine	Cam machine
1	Chest	12-15	2	Bench press	Bench press	Chest press
2	Back	12-15	2	One-arm dumbbell row	Lat pulldown	Machine pullover
3	Shoulders	12-15	2	Standing press	Seated press	Shoulder press
4	Front of arm	12-15	2	Biceps curl	Low pulley curl	Preacher curl
5	Back of arm	12-15	2	Dumbbell triceps extension	Triceps pushdown	Triceps extension
6	Thighs	12-15	2	Lunge	Leg press	Horizontal leg press
7	Abdomen	12-15	2	Sit-up	Abdominal crunch	Abdominal crunch

Rest period: 30 seconds

Cool-down: Slow walking for 5 minutes followed by stretching

Workout tips

* Complete one set of each exercise and then start over and perform the second set of each exercise (as opposed to doing two sets of each exercise back to back).

Level 1   Workout 3

Total time: 51 minutes

Weeks: 5 and 6

Days of the week: Two nonconsecutive days

Warm-up: Easy jogging or rope skipping for 5 minutes followed by stretching

Exercises: 21 minutes

Number	Muscle group	Reps	Sets*	Free weight	Pivot machine	Cam machine
1	Chest	12-15	2	Bench press	Bench press	Chest press
2	Back	12-15	2	One-arm dumbbell row	Lat pulldown	Machine pullover
3	Shoulders	12-15	2	Standing press	Seated press	Shoulder press
4	Front of arm	12-15	2	Biceps curl	Low pulley curl	Preacher curl
5	Back of arm	12-15	2	Dumbbell triceps extension	Triceps pushdown	Triceps extension
6	Thighs	12-15	2	Lunge	Leg press	Horizontal leg press
7	Abdomen	12-15	2	Sit-up	Abdominal crunch	Abdominal crunch

Rest period: 30 seconds

Cool-down: Slow walking for 5 minutes followed by stretching

Workout tips

   * At this point you should be able to perform the required two sets back to back.

Level 2 Workout 1

Total time: 56 minutes

Weeks: 1 and 2

Days of the week: Two nonconsecutive days

Warm-up: Easy jogging or rope skipping for 5 minutes followed by stretching

Exercises: 26 minutes

Number	Muscle group	Reps	Sets*	Free weight	Pivot machine	Cam machine
1	Chest	12-15	3**	Bench press	Bench press	Chest press
2	Back	12-15	2	One-arm dumbbell row	Lat pulldown	Machine pullover
3	Shoulders	12-15	3**	Standing press	Seated press	Shoulder press
4	Front of arm	12-15	2	Biceps curl	Low pulley curl	Preacher curl
5	Back of arm	12-15	2	Dumbbell triceps extension	Triceps pushdown	Triceps extension
6	Thighs	12-15	3**	Lunge	Leg press	Horizontal leg press
7	Abdomen	12-15	2	Sit-up	Abdominal crunch	Abdominal crunch

Rest period: 30 seconds

Cool-down: Slow walking for 5 minutes followed by stretching

Workout tips

* Do two sets of each exercise back to back.

** After doing two sets of all exercises, come back and perform the last (third) set of exercises 1, 3, and 6 in this order: 1, 6, and then 3.

Level 2   Workout 2

Total time: 56 minutes

Weeks: 3 and 4

Days of the week: Two nonconsecutive days

Warm-up: Easy jogging or rope skipping for 5 minutes followed by stretching

Exercises: 26 minutes

Number	Muscle group	Reps	Sets*	Free weight	Pivot machine	Cam machine
1	Chest	12-15	3	Bench press	Bench press	Chest press
2	Back	12-15	2	One-arm dumbbell row	Lat pulldown	Machine pullover
3	Shoulders	12-15	3	Standing press	Seated press	Shoulder press
4	Front of arm	12-15	2	Biceps curl	Low pulley curl	Preacher curl
5	Back of arm	12-15	2	Dumbbell triceps extension	Triceps pushdown	Triceps extension
6	Thighs	12-15	3	Lunge	Leg press	Horizontal leg press
7	Abdomen	12-15	2	Sit-up	Abdominal crunch	Abdominal crunch

Rest period: 30 seconds

Cool-down: Slow walking for 5 minutes followed by stretching

Workout tips

   * At this point you should be able to perform the required two or three sets back to back.

Level 2   Workout 3

Total time: 1 hour, 2 minutes

Weeks: 5 and 6

Days of the week: Two nonconsecutive days

Warm-up: Easy jogging or rope skipping for 5 minutes followed by stretching

Exercises: 32 minutes

Number	Muscle group	Reps	Sets*	Free weight	Pivot machine	Cam machine
1	Chest	12-15	3	Bench press	Bench press	Chest press
2	Back	12-15	3	One-arm dumbbell row	Lat pulldown	Machine pullover
3	Shoulders	12-15	3	Standing press	Seated press	Shoulder press
4	Front of arm	12-15	3	Biceps curl	Low pulley curl	Preacher curl
5	Back of arm	12-15	3	Dumbbell triceps extension	Triceps pushdown	Triceps extension
6	Thighs	12-15	3	Lunge	Leg press	Horizontal leg press
7	Abdomen	12-15	3	Sit-up	Abdominal crunch	Abdominal crunch

Rest period: 30 seconds

Cool-down: Slow walking for 5 minutes followed by stretching

Workout tips

  * At this point you should be able to perform the required three sets back to back.

Level 3   Workout 1

Total time: 51 minutes

Weeks: 1 and 2

Days of the week: Three nonconsecutive days*

Warm-up: Easy jogging or rope skipping for 5 minutes followed by stretching

Exercises: 21 minutes

Number	Muscle group	Reps	Sets	Free weight	Pivot machine	Cam machine
1	Chest	12-15	2	Bench press	Bench press	Chest press
2	Back	12-15	2	One-arm dumbbell row	Lat pulldown	Machine pullover
3	Shoulders	12-15	2	Standing press	Seated press	Shoulder press
4	Front of arm	12-15	2	Biceps curl	Low pulley curl	Preacher curl
5	Back of arm	12-15	2	Dumbbell triceps extension	Triceps pushdown	Triceps extension
6	Thighs	12-15	2	Lunge	Leg press	Horizontal leg press
7	Abdomen	15-25**	2	Sit-up	Abdominal crunch	Abdominal crunch

Rest period: 30 seconds

Cool-down: Slow walking for 5 minutes followed by stretching

Workout tips

* Be sure to spread out your weight training sessions throughout the week; you need at least one rest day (but no more than three) between workouts. A common three-days-per-week program is Monday, Wednesday, and Friday or Tuesday, Thursday, and one weekend day.

** Note that you are now doing sets of 15 to 25 reps for your abdominal exercise.

Level 3   Workout 2

Total time: 56 minutes

Weeks: 3 and 4

Days of the week: Three nonconsecutive days

Warm-up: Easy jogging or rope skipping for 5 minutes followed by stretching

Exercises: 26 minutes

Number	Muscle group	Reps	Sets*	Free weight	Pivot machine	Cam machine
1	Chest	12-15	3**	Bench press	Bench press	Chest press
2	Back	12-15	2	One-arm dumbbell row	Lat pulldown	Machine pullover
3	Shoulders	12-15	3**	Standing press	Seated press	Shoulder press
4	Front of arm	12-15	2	Biceps curl	Low pulley curl	Preacher curl
5	Back of arm	12-15	2	Dumbbell triceps extension	Triceps pushdown	Triceps extension
6	Thighs	12-15	3**	Lunge	Leg press	Horizontal leg press
7	Abdomen	15-25	2	Sit-up	Abdominal crunch	Abdominal crunch

Rest period: 30 seconds

Cool-down: Slow walking for 5 minutes followed by stretching

Workout tips

   * Do two sets of each exercise back to back.

   ** After doing two sets of all exercises, come back and perform the last (third) set of exercises 1, 3, and 6 in this order: 1, 6, and then 3.

Level 3   Workout 3

Total time: 56 minutes

Weeks: 5 and 6

Days of the week: Three nonconsecutive days

Warm-up: Easy jogging or rope skipping for 5 minutes followed by stretching

Exercises: 26 minutes

Number	Muscle group	Reps	Sets*	Free weight	Pivot machine	Cam machine
1	Chest	12-15	3	Bench press	Bench press	Chest press
2	Back	12-15	2	One-arm dumbbell row	Lat pulldown	Machine pullover
3	Shoulders	12-15	3	Standing press	Seated press	Shoulder press
4	Front of arm	12-15	2	Biceps curl	Low pulley curl	Preacher curl
5	Back of arm	12-15	2	Dumbbell triceps extension	Triceps pushdown	Triceps extension
6	Thighs	12-15	3	Lunge	Leg press	Horizontal leg press
7	Abdomen	15-25	2	Sit-up	Abdominal crunch	Abdominal crunch

Rest period: 30 seconds

Cool-down: Slow walking for 5 minutes followed by stretching

Workout tips

*   At this point you should be able to perform the required two or three sets back to back.

Level 4   Workout 1

Total time: 1 hour, 2 minutes

Weeks: 1 and 2

Days of the week: Three nonconsecutive days

Warm-up: Easy jogging or rope skipping for 5 minutes followed by stretching

Exercises: 32 minutes

Number	Muscle group	Reps	Sets	Free weight	Pivot machine	Cam machine
1	Chest	12-15	3	Bench press	Bench press	Chest press
2	Back	12-15	3	One-arm dumbbell row	Lat pulldown	Machine pullover
3	Shoulders	12-15	3	Standing press	Seated press	Shoulder press
4	Front of arm	12-15	3	Biceps curl	Low pulley curl	Preacher curl
5	Back of arm	12-15	3	Dumbbell triceps extension	Triceps pushdown	Triceps extension
6	Thighs	12-15	3	Lunge	Leg press	Horizontal leg press
7	Abdomen	15-25	3	Sit-up	Abdominal crunch	Abdominal crunch

Rest period: 30 seconds*

Cool-down: Slow walking for 5 minutes followed by stretching

Workout tips

  * You can add a challenging element to your program as your training status improves by slightly decreasing the rest time to 20 seconds between sets or exercises.

Level 4   Workout 2

Total time: 1 hour, 6 minutes

Weeks: 3 and 4

Days of the week: Three nonconsecutive days

Warm-up: Easy jogging or rope skipping for 5 minutes followed by stretching

Exercises: 36 minutes

Number	Muscle group	Reps	Sets	Free weight	Pivot machine	Cam machine
1	Chest	12-15	3	Bench press	Bench press	Chest press
2*	Chest	12-15	1**	Dumbbell fly	Pec deck	Pec deck
3	Back	12-15	3	One-arm dumbbell row	Lat pulldown	Machine pullover
4	Shoulder	12-15	3	Standing press	Seated press	Shoulder press
5*	Back	12-15	1**	Bent-over row	Seated row	Lat pulldown
6	Back of arm	12-15	3	Dumbbell triceps extension	Triceps pushdown	Triceps extension
7	Front of arm	12-15	3	Biceps curl	Low pulley curl	Preacher curl
8	Thigh	12-15	3	Lunge	Leg press	Horizontal leg press
9	Abdomen	15-25	3	Sit-up	Abdominal crunch	Abdominal crunch
10*	Calf	12-15	1**	Standing heel raise	Standing heel raise	Machine standing heel raise

Rest period: 30 seconds

Cool-down: Slow walking for 5 minutes followed by stretching

Workout tips

* Now you are completing 10 exercises per session; to learn how to perform your new exercises, consult chapter 10. The procedure described in chapter 5 will help you determine your starting loads in these exercises.

** For these two weeks, perform the one set of exercises 2, 5, and 10 after completing all the other exercises.

Level 4 Workout 3

Total time: 1 hour, 6 minutes

Weeks: 5 and 6

Days of the week: Three nonconsecutive days

Warm-up: Easy jogging or rope skipping for 5 minutes followed by stretching

Exercises: 36 minutes

Number*	Muscle group	Reps	Sets	Free weight	Pivot machine	Cam machine
1	Chest	12-15	3	Bench press	Bench press	Chest press
2	Chest	12-15	1	Dumbbell fly	Pec deck	Pec deck
3	Back	12-15	3	One-arm dumbbell row	Lat pulldown	Machine pullover
4	Shoulder	12-15	3	Standing press	Seated press	Shoulder press
5	Back	12-15	1	Bent-over row	Seated row	Lat pulldown
6	Back of arm	12-15	3	Dumbbell triceps extension	Triceps pushdown	Triceps extension
7	Front of arm	12-15	3	Biceps curl	Low pulley curl	Preacher curl
8	Thigh	12-15	3	Lunge	Leg press	Horizontal leg press
9	Abdomen	15-25	3	Sit-up	Abdominal crunch	Abdominal crunch
10	Calf	12-15	1	Standing heel raise	Standing heel raise	Machine standing heel raise

Rest period: 30 seconds

Cool-down: Slow walking for 5 minutes followed by stretching

Workout tips

  * Perform all exercises in the order listed.

Level 5   Workout 1

Total time: 1 hour, 11 minutes

Weeks: 1 and 2

Days of the week: Three nonconsecutive days

Warm-up: Easy jogging or rope skipping for 5 minutes followed by stretching

Exercises: 41 minutes

Number	Muscle group	Reps	Sets	Free weight	Pivot machine	Cam machine
1	Chest	12-15	3	Bench press	Bench press	Chest press
2	Chest	12-15	2*	Dumbbell fly	Pec deck	Pec deck
3	Back	12-15	3	One-arm dumbbell row	Lat pulldown	Machine pullover
4	Shoulder	12-15	3	Standing press	Seated press	Shoulder press
5	Back	12-15	2*	Bent-over row	Seated row	Lat pulldown
6	Back of arm	12-15	3	Dumbbell triceps extension	Triceps pushdown	Triceps extension
7	Front of arm	12-15	3	Biceps curl	Low pulley curl	Preacher curl
8	Thigh	12-15	3	Lunge	Leg press	Horizontal leg press
9	Abdomen	15-25	3	Sit-up	Abdominal crunch	Abdominal crunch
10	Calf	12-15	2*	Standing heel raise	Standing heel raise	Machine standing heel raise

Rest period: 30 seconds

Cool-down: Slow walking for 5 minutes followed by stretching

Workout tips

   * At this point, you should be able to perform the required two sets back to back.

Level 5 Workout 2

Total time: 1 hour, 15 minutes

Weeks: 3 and 4

Days of the week: Three nonconsecutive days

Warm-up: Easy jogging or rope skipping for 5 minutes followed by stretching

Exercises: 45 minutes

Number	Muscle group	Reps	Sets	Free weight	Pivot machine	Cam machine
1	Chest	12-15	3	Bench press	Bench press	Chest press
2	Chest	12-15	3*	Dumbbell fly	Pec deck	Pec deck
3	Back	12-15	3	One-arm dumbbell row	Lat pulldown	Machine pullover
4	Shoulder	12-15	3	Standing press	Seated press	Shoulder press
5	Back	12-15	3	Bent-over row	Seated row	Lat pulldown
6	Back of arm	12-15	3	Dumbbell triceps extension	Triceps pushdown	Triceps extension
7	Front of arm	12-15	3	Biceps curl	Low pulley curl	Preacher curl
8	Thigh	12-15	3	Lunge	Leg press	Horizontal leg press
9	Abdomen	15-25	3	Sit-up	Abdominal crunch	Abdominal crunch
10	Calf	12-15	3	Standing heel raise	Standing heel raise	Machine standing heel raise

Rest period: 30 seconds

Cool-down: Slow walking for 5 minutes followed by stretching

Workout tips

> * Because this program contains three sets of two chest exercises listed in order, you may need to readjust the load that you are using in exercise 2 to complete three back-to-back sets.

Level 5 Workout 3

Total time: 1 hour, 26 minutes

Weeks: 5 and 6

Days of the week: Three nonconsecutive days

Warm-up: Easy jogging or rope skipping for 5 minutes followed by stretching

Exercises: 56 minutes

Number	Muscle group	Reps	Sets	Free weight	Pivot machine	Cam machine
1	Chest	12-15	4*	Bench press	Bench press	Chest press
2	Chest	12-15	3	Dumbbell fly	Pec deck	Pec deck
3	Back	12-15	4*	One-arm dumbbell row	Lat pulldown	Machine pullover
4	Shoulder	12-15	4*	Standing press	Seated press	Shoulder press
5	Back	12-15	3	Bent-over row	Seated row	Lat pulldown
6	Back of arm	12-15	4*	Dumbbell triceps extension	Triceps pushdown	Triceps extension
7	Front of arm	12-15	4*	Biceps curl	Low pulley curl	Preacher curl
8	Thigh	12-15	4*	Lunge	Leg press	Horizontal leg press
9	Abdomen	15-25	4*	Sit-up	Abdominal crunch	Abdominal crunch
10	Calf	12-15	3	Standing heel raise	Standing heel raise	Machine standing heel raise

Rest period: 30 seconds

Cool-down: Slow walking for 5 minutes followed by stretching

Workout tips

* As you begin performing four sets in these exercises, you may have to decrease the load slightly (5 to 10 pounds for exercises 1, 3, 4, and 6 through 9 and 10 to 15 pounds for exercise 8) to allow you to complete all four sets successfully.

Level 6   Workout 1

Total time: 1 hour, 30 minutes
Weeks: 1 and 2
Days of the week: Three nonconsecutive days
Warm-up: Easy jogging or rope skipping for 5 minutes followed by stretching
Exercises: 1 hour

Number	Muscle group	Reps	Sets	Free weight	Pivot machine	Cam machine
1	Chest	12-15	4	Bench press	Bench press	Chest press
2	Chest	12-15	3	Dumbbell fly	Pec deck	Pec deck
3	Back	12-15	4	One-arm dumbbell row	Lat pulldown	Machine pullover
4	Shoulder	12-15	4	Standing press	Seated press	Shoulder press
5	Back	12-15	3	Bent-over row	Seated row	Lat pulldown
6*	Shoulder	12-15	1**	Dumbbell lateral raise	Machine lateral raise	Machine lateral raise
7	Back of arm	12-15	4	Dumbbell triceps extension	Triceps pushdown	Triceps extension
8	Front of arm	12-15	4	Biceps curl	Low pulley curl	Preacher curl
9	Thigh	12-15	4	Lunge	Leg press	Horizontal leg press
10*	Back of thigh	12-15	1**	Leg (knee) curl	Leg (knee) curl	Leg (knee) curl
11*	Front of thigh	12-15	1**	Leg (knee) extension	Leg (knee) extension	Leg (knee) extension
12	Abdomen	15-25	4	Sit-up	Abdominal crunch	Abdominal crunch
13	Calf	12-15	3	Standing heel raise	Standing heel raise	Machine standing heel raise

Rest period: 30 seconds

Cool-down: Slow walking for 5 minutes followed by stretching

Workout tips

* Now you are completing 13 exercises per session; to learn how to perform your new exercises, consult chapter 10. The procedure described in chapter 5 will help you determine your starting loads in these exercises.

** Be sure to perform the new exercises (6, 10, and 11) in the order listed.

Level 6 Workout 2

Total time: 1 hour, 35 minutes

Weeks: 3 and 4

Days of the week: Three nonconsecutive days

Warm-up: Easy jogging or rope skipping for 5 minutes followed by stretching

Exercises: 1 hour, 5 minutes

Number	Muscle group	Reps	Sets	Free weight	Pivot machine	Cam machine
1	Chest	12-15	4	Bench press	Bench press	Chest press
2	Chest	12-15	3	Dumbbell fly	Pec deck	Pec deck
3	Back	12-15	4	One-arm dumbbell row	Lat pulldown	Machine pullover
4	Shoulder	12-15	4	Standing press	Seated press	Shoulder press
5	Back	12-15	3	Bent-over row	Seated row	Lat pulldown
6	Shoulder	12-15	2*	Dumbbell lateral raise	Machine lateral raise	Machine lateral raise
7	Back of arm	12-15	4	Dumbbell triceps extension	Triceps pushdown	Triceps extension
8	Front of arm	12-15	4	Biceps curl	Low pulley curl	Preacher curl
9	Thigh	12-15	4	Lunge	Leg press	Horizontal leg press
10	Back of thigh	12-15	2*	Leg (knee) curl	Leg (knee) curl	Leg (knee) curl
11	Front of thigh	12-15	2*	Leg (knee) extension	Leg (knee) extension	Leg (knee) extension
12	Abdomen	15-25	4	Sit-up	Abdominal crunch	Abdominal crunch
13	Calf	12-15	3	Standing heel raise	Standing heel raise	Machine standing heel raise

Rest period: 30 seconds

Cool-down: Slow walking for 5 minutes followed by stretching

Workout tips

   * Be sure to perform the new exercises (6, 10, and 11) in the order listed.

Level 6   Workout 3

Total time: 1 hour, 39 minutes

Weeks: 5 and 6

Days of the week: Three nonconsecutive days

Warm-up: Easy jogging or rope skipping for 5 minutes followed by stretching

Exercises: 1 hour, 9 minutes

Number	Muscle group	Reps	Sets	Free weight	Pivot machine	Cam machine
1	Chest	12-15	4	Bench press	Bench press	Chest press
2	Chest	12-15	3	Dumbbell fly	Pec deck	Pec deck
3	Back	12-15	4	One-arm dumbbell row	Lat pulldown	Machine pullover
4	Shoulder	12-15	4	Standing press	Seated press	Shoulder press
5	Back	12-15	3	Bent-over row	Seated row	Lat pulldown
6	Shoulder	12-15	3*	Dumbbell lateral raise	Machine lateral raise	Machine lateral raise
7	Back of arm	12-15	4	Dumbbell triceps extension	Triceps pushdown	Triceps extension
8	Front of arm	12-15	4	Biceps curl	Low pulley curl	Preacher curl
9	Thigh	12-15	4	Lunge	Leg press	Horizontal leg press
10	Back of thigh	12-15	3*	Leg (knee) curl	Leg (knee) curl	Leg (knee) curl
11	Front of thigh	12-15	3*	Leg (knee) extension	Leg (knee) extension	Leg (knee) extension
12	Abdomen	15-25	4	Sit-up	Abdominal crunch	Abdominal crunch
13	Calf	12-15	3	Standing heel raise	Standing heel raise	Machine standing heel raise

Rest period: 30 seconds

Cool-down: Slow walking for 5 minutes followed by stretching

Workout tips

   * Be sure to perform the sets for exercises 6, 10, and 11 back to back and in the order listed.

8

Body Shaping

Body-shaping programs result in many of the same changes produced by muscle-toning programs, but they also can make the trained muscle larger (primarily in men). Women's bodies usually do not respond in the same way, although the shoulders, thighs, arms, or back of some women may become a bit more muscular. Commonly, though, this type of weight training program will be effective at sculpting or reproportioning the body in a pleasing way.

Training-Goal Highlights

Level 1

- The body-shaping program begins with three workouts per week that consist of one set of 12 to 15 reps for seven exercises. The program includes an exercise for each major muscle group: chest, back, shoulders, front of the upper arm (biceps), back of the upper arm (triceps), thighs, and abdomen.

- The number of sets increases from one to two in the third week, and by the fifth week, you perform those two sets back to back.

Level 2

- The body-shaping program gradually decreases the number of reps to 10 to 12 but retains three sessions a week. Remember, as the number of reps decreases, you should increase the loads (chapter 5 can assist you in this process).

Level 3

- The six weeks of this level gradually train you to be able to perform 10 to 12 reps in three back-to-back sets for the seven original exercises.

Level 4

- A major change in level 4 is that you will be completing four workouts each week; your program is divided into two upper-body and two lower-body training days. Because of the increase in the number of weekly workouts, weeks 1 and 2 will require only one set of 10 to 12 reps in the two new upper-body exercises and the four new lower-body exercises. The upper-body exercises include two each for the chest and back and one each for the shoulders, front of the upper arm (biceps), and back of the upper arm (triceps). The lower-body exercises include two for the thighs and one each for the back of the thigh (hamstrings), the front of the thigh (quadriceps), the calves, and the abdomen. Chapter 5 will help you determine the loads for your new exercises.
- Weeks 3 through 6 gradually return you to three back-to-back sets in each of your seven upper-body and six lower-body exercises.

Level 5

- For your upper-body workouts, weeks 1 and 2 add three exercises— one set of 10 to 12 reps each for your shoulders, upper arm (biceps), and back of the upper arm (triceps).
- For your lower-body workouts, weeks 1 and 2 add two exercises—one set of 10 to 12 reps each for your thighs and calves.
- To determine what loads you should use in the new exercises, follow the guidelines in chapter 5.
- Weeks 3 through 6 gradually add sets so that you finish level 5 with three back-to-back sets in each of your 10 upper-body and 8 lower-body exercises.

Level 6

- Weeks 1 and 2 decrease the number of reps to 8 to 10 in the third set (only) of the two major upper-body exercises (a chest exercise and a shoulder exercise) and in the two major lower-body exercises (both thigh exercises). Be sure to increase the weight slightly for these exercises (see chapter 5).
- Weeks 3 and 4 require that you perform two of the three sets in the four major exercises with a slightly heavier weight for 8 to 10 reps.
- Weeks 5 and 6 add one set of 10 to 12 reps (now you will be doing a total of four) in the four major exercises.
- By the end of week 6 of level 6, you will be performing three to four sets of 8 to 12 repetitions in 10 upper-body and 8 lower-body exercises during four workouts per week!

Level 1   Workout 1

Total time: 44 minutes

Weeks: 1 and 2

Days of the week: Three nonconsecutive days*

Warm-up: Easy jogging or rope skipping for 5 minutes followed by stretching

Exercises: 14 minutes

Number	Muscle group	Reps	Sets	Free weight	Pivot machine	Cam machine
1	Chest	12-15	1	Bench press	Bench press	Chest press
2	Back	12-15	1	Bent-over row	Seated row	Seated row
3	Shoulders	12-15	1	Standing press	Seated press	Shoulder press
4	Front of arm	12-15	1	Biceps curl	Low pulley curl	Preacher curl
5	Back of arm	12-15	1	Dumbbell triceps extension	Triceps pushdown	Triceps extension
6	Thighs	12-15	1	Lunge	Leg press	Horizontal leg press
7	Abdomen	12-15	1	Sit-up	Abdominal crunch	Abdominal crunch

Rest period: 30 seconds**

Cool-down: Slow walking for 5 minutes followed by stretching

Workout tips

   * Be sure to spread out your weight training sessions throughout the week; you need at least one rest day (but no more than three) between workouts. A common three-days-per-week program is Monday, Wednesday, and Friday or Tuesday, Thursday, and one weekend day.

  ** You may want to rest for up to 60 seconds between exercises for your first or second week of training, or both.

Level 1   Workout 2

Total time: 51 minutes

Weeks: 3 and 4

Days of the week: Three nonconsecutive days

Warm-up: Easy jogging or rope skipping for 5 minutes followed by stretching

Exercises: 21 minutes

Number	Muscle group	Reps	Sets*	Free weight	Pivot machine	Cam machine
1	Chest	12-15	2	Bench press	Bench press	Chest press
2	Back	12-15	2	Bent-over row	Seated row	Seated row
3	Shoulders	12-15	2	Standing press	Seated press	Shoulder press
4	Front of arm	12-15	2	Biceps curl	Low pulley curl	Preacher curl
5	Back of arm	12-15	2	Dumbbell triceps extension	Triceps pushdown	Triceps extension
6	Thighs	12-15	2	Lunge	Leg press	Horizontal leg press
7	Abdomen	12-15	2	Sit-up	Abdominal crunch	Abdominal crunch

Rest period: 30 seconds

Cool-down: Slow walking for 5 minutes followed by stretching

Workout tips

* Complete one set of each exercise and then start over and perform the second set of each exercise (as opposed to doing two sets of each exercise back to back).

Level 1   Workout 3

Total time: 51 minutes

Weeks: 5 and 6

Days of the week: Three nonconsecutive days

Warm-up: Easy jogging or rope skipping for 5 minutes followed by stretching

Exercises: 21 minutes

Number	Muscle group	Reps	Sets*	Free weight	Pivot machine	Cam machine
1	Chest	12-15	2	Bench press	Bench press	Chest press
2	Back	12-15	2	Bent-over row	Seated row	Seated row
3	Shoulders	12-15	2	Standing press	Seated press	Shoulder press
4	Front of arm	12-15	2	Biceps curl	Low pulley curl	Preacher curl
5	Back of arm	12-15	2	Dumbbell triceps extension	Triceps pushdown	Triceps extension
6	Thighs	12-15	2	Lunge	Leg press	Horizontal leg press
7	Abdomen	12-15	2	Sit-up	Abdominal crunch	Abdominal crunch

Rest period: 30 seconds

Cool-down: Slow walking for 5 minutes followed by stretching

Workout tips

* At this point you should be able to perform the required two sets back to back.

Level 2   Workout 1

Total time: 52 minutes

Weeks: 1 and 2

Days of the week: Three nonconsecutive days

Warm-up: Easy jogging or rope skipping for 5 minutes followed by stretching

Exercises: 22 minutes

Number	Muscle group	Reps	Sets	Free weight	Pivot machine	Cam machine
1	Chest	12-15 10-12*	1 1	Bench press	Bench press	Chest press
2	Back	12-15	2	Bent-over row	Seated row	Seated row
3	Shoulders	12-15 10-12*	1 1	Standing press	Seated press	Shoulder press
4	Front of arm	12-15	2	Biceps curl	Low pulley curl	Preacher curl
5	Back of arm	12-15	2	Dumbbell triceps extension	Triceps pushdown	Triceps extension
6	Thighs	12-15 10-12*	1 1	Lunge	Leg press	Horizontal leg press
7	Abdomen	15-25**	2	Sit-up	Abdominal crunch	Abdominal crunch

Rest period: 60 seconds after sets of 10 to 12 repetitions***; 30 seconds after sets of 12 to 15 repetitions

Cool-down: Slow walking for 5 minutes followed by stretching

Workout tips

  * When you make the change to performing sets of 10 to 12 repetitions instead of 12 to 15 repetitions, a general guideline is to add 5 to 10 pounds to your upper-body exercises and 10 to 20 pounds to your lower-body exercises. At this point you only have to lift the heavier weight (and perform fewer repetitions) in the second of the two sets for exercises 1, 3, and 6.

  ** You are now doing sets of 15 to 25 reps for your abdominal exercise.

  *** The rest period after these heavier sets is longer (60 seconds versus 30 seconds).

Level 2   Workout 2

Total time: 53 minutes

Weeks: 3 and 4

Days of the week: Three nonconsecutive days

Warm-up: Easy jogging or rope skipping for 5 minutes followed by stretching

Exercises: 23 minutes

Number	Muscle group	Reps	Sets	Free weight	Pivot machine	Cam machine
1	Chest	10-12	2*	Bench press	Bench press	Chest press
2	Back	12-15	2	Bent-over row	Seated row	Seated row
3	Shoulders	10-12	2*	Standing press	Seated press	Shoulder press
4	Front of arm	12-15	2	Biceps curl	Low pulley curl	Preacher curl
5	Back of arm	12-15	2	Dumbbell triceps extension	Triceps pushdown	Triceps extension
6	Thighs	10-12	2*	Lunge	Leg press	Horizontal leg press
7	Abdomen	15-25	2	Sit-up	Abdominal crunch	Abdominal crunch

Rest period: 60 seconds for exercises 1, 3, and 6; 30 seconds for exercises 2, 4, 5, and 7

Cool-down: Slow walking for 5 minutes followed by stretching

Workout tips

* As you begin performing both sets with the heavier load (for fewer repetitions) for exercises 1, 3, and 6, you may have to decrease the load slightly in the second set to complete both sets successfully.

Level 2 Workout 3

Total time: 55 minutes

Weeks: 5 and 6

Days of the week: Three nonconsecutive days

Warm-up: Easy jogging or rope skipping for 5 minutes followed by stretching

Exercises: 25 minutes

Number	Muscle group	Reps	Sets	Free weight	Pivot machine	Cam machine
1	Chest	10-12	2	Bench press	Bench press	Chest press
2	Back	10-12*	2**	Bent-over row	Seated row	Seated row
3	Shoulders	10-12	2	Standing press	Seated press	Shoulder press
4	Front of arm	10-12*	2**	Biceps curl	Low pulley curl	Preacher curl
5	Back of arm	10-12*	2**	Dumbbell triceps extension	Triceps pushdown	Triceps extension
6	Thighs	10-12	2	Lunge	Leg press	Horizontal leg press
7	Abdomen	15-25	2	Sit-up	Abdominal crunch	Abdominal crunch

Rest period: 1 minute

Cool-down: Slow walking for 5 minutes followed by stretching

Workout tips

* When you make the change to performing sets of 10 to 12 repetitions instead of 12 to 15 repetitions for exercises 2, 4, and 5, a general guideline is to add 5 to 10 pounds to your upper-body exercises and 10 to 20 pounds to your lower-body exercises.

** As you begin performing both sets with the heavier load (for fewer repetitions), you may have to decrease the load slightly in the second set to complete both sets successfully.

Level 3   Workout 1

Total time: 1 hour, 1 minute

Weeks: 1 and 2

Days of the week: Three nonconsecutive days

Warm-up: Easy jogging or rope skipping for 5 minutes followed by stretching

Exercises: 31 minutes

Number	Muscle group	Reps	Sets	Free weight	Pivot machine	Cam machine
1	Chest	10-12	3*	Bench press	Bench press	Chest press
2	Back	10-12	2	Bent-over row	Seated row	Seated row
3	Shoulders	10-12	3*	Standing press	Seated press	Shoulder press
4	Front of arm	10-12	2	Biceps curl	Low pulley curl	Preacher curl
5	Back of arm	10-12	2	Dumbbell triceps extension	Triceps pushdown	Triceps extension
6	Thighs	10-12	3*	Lunge	Leg press	Horizontal leg press
7	Abdomen	15-25	2	Sit-up	Abdominal crunch	Abdominal crunch

Rest period: 1 minute

Cool-down: Slow walking for 5 minutes followed by stretching

Workout tips

* Do two sets of each exercise back to back and then come back and perform the last (third) set of exercises 1, 3, and 6 in this order: 1, 6, and then 3.

Level 3   Workout 2

Total time: 1 hour, 1 minute

Weeks: 3 and 4

Days of the week: Three nonconsecutive days

Warm-up: Easy jogging or rope skipping for 5 minutes followed by stretching

Exercises: 31 minutes

Number	Muscle group	Reps	Sets*	Free weight	Pivot machine	Cam machine
1	Chest	10-12	3	Bench press	Bench press	Chest press
2	Back	10-12	2	Bent-over row	Seated row	Seated row
3	Shoulders	10-12	3	Standing press	Seated press	Shoulder press
4	Front of arm	10-12	2	Biceps curl	Low pulley curl	Preacher curl
5	Back of arm	10-12	2	Dumbbell triceps extension	Triceps pushdown	Triceps extension
6	Thighs	10-12	3	Lunge	Leg press	Horizontal leg press
7	Abdomen	15-25	2	Sit-up	Abdominal crunch	Abdominal crunch

Rest period: 1 minute

Cool-down: Slow walking for 5 minutes followed by stretching

Workout tips

   * At this point you should be able to perform the required two or three sets back to back.

Level 3   Workout 3

Total time: 1 hour, 8 minutes
Weeks: 5 and 6
Days of the week: Three nonconsecutive days
Warm-up: Easy jogging or rope skipping for 5 minutes followed by stretching
Exercises: 38 minutes

Number	Muscle group	Reps	Sets*	Free weight	Pivot machine	Cam machine
1	Chest	10-12	3	Bench press	Bench press	Chest press
2	Back	10-12	3	Bent-over row	Seated row	Seated row
3	Shoulders	10-12	3	Standing press	Seated press	Shoulder press
4	Front of arm	10-12	3	Biceps curl	Low pulley curl	Preacher curl
5	Back of arm	10-12	3	Dumbbell triceps extension	Triceps pushdown	Triceps extension
6	Thighs	10-12	3	Lunge	Leg press	Horizontal leg press
7	Abdomen	15-25	3	Sit-up	Abdominal crunch	Abdominal crunch

Rest period: 1 minute

Cool-down: Slow walking for 5 minutes followed by stretching

Workout tips

   * At this point you should be able to perform the required three sets back to back.

Level 4   Workout 1

Total time: 1 hour, 1 minute

Weeks: 1 and 2

Days of the week: Two nonconsecutive days*

Warm-up: Easy jogging or rope skipping for 5 minutes followed by stretching

Upper-body exercises: 31 minutes

Number	Muscle group	Reps	Sets	Free weight	Pivot machine	Cam machine
1	Chest	10-12	3	Bench press	Bench press	Chest press
2**	Chest	10-12	1	Dumbbell fly	Pec deck	Pec deck
3	Back	10-12	3	Bent-over row	Seated row	Seated row
4	Shoulder	10-12	3	Standing press	Seated press	Shoulder press
5**	Back	10-12	1	One-arm dumbbell row	Lat pulldown	Machine pullover
6	Back of arm	10-12	3	Dumbbell triceps extension	Triceps pushdown	Triceps extension
7	Front of arm	10-12	3	Biceps curl	Low pulley curl	Preacher curl

Rest period: 1 minute

Cool-down: Slow walking for 5 minutes followed by stretching

Workout tips

* When you make the change to four workouts per week, you will perform upper-body and lower-body workouts separately, allowing you to add new exercises and still complete your workouts in about the same amount of time. A common program schedules upper-body exercises on Mondays and Thursdays and lower-body exercises on Tuesdays and Fridays.

** Refer to chapter 5 to determine your starting loads for new exercises and chapter 10 to learn how to perform them correctly.

Level 4   Workout 2

Total time: 48 minutes

Weeks: 1 and 2

Days of the week: Two nonconsecutive days*

Warm-up: Easy jogging or rope skipping for 5 minutes followed by stretching

Lower-body exercises: 18 minutes

Number	Muscle group	Reps	Sets	Free weight	Pivot machine	Cam machine
1**	Thighs	10-12	1	Squat	Leg press	Horizontal leg press
2	Thighs	10-12	3	Lunge	Leg press	Horizontal leg press
3**	Back of thigh	10-12	1	Leg (knee) curl	Leg (knee) curl	Leg (knee) curl
4**	Front of thigh	10-12	1	Leg (knee) extension	Leg (knee) extension	Leg (knee) extension
5**	Calf	10-12	1	Standing heel raise	Seated heel raise	Machine standing heel raise
6	Abdomen	15-25	3	Sit-up	Abdominal crunch	Abdominal crunch

Rest period: 1 minute

Cool-down: Slow walking for 5 minutes followed by stretching

Workout tips

* When you make the change to four workouts per week, you will perform upper-body and lower-body workouts separately, allowing you to add new exercises and still complete your workouts in about the same amount of time. A common program schedules upper-body exercises on Mondays and Thursdays and lower-body exercises on Tuesdays and Fridays.

** Refer to chapter 5 to determine your starting loads for new exercises and chapter 10 to learn how to perform them correctly.

Level 4   Workout 3

Total time: 1 hour, 4 minutes

Weeks: 3 and 4

Days of the week: Two nonconsecutive days

Warm-up: Easy jogging or rope skipping for 5 minutes followed by stretching

Upper-body exercises: 34 minutes

Number	Muscle group	Reps	Sets	Free weight	Pivot machine	Cam machine
1	Chest	10-12	3	Bench press	Bench press	Chest press
2	Chest	10-12	2*	Dumbbell fly	Pec deck	Pec deck
3	Back	10-12	3	Bent-over row	Seated row	Seated row
4	Shoulder	10-12	3	Standing press	Seated press	Shoulder press
5	Back	10-12	2*	One-arm dumbbell row	Lat pulldown	Machine pullover
6	Back of arm	10-12	3	Dumbbell triceps extension	Triceps pushdown	Triceps extension
7	Front of arm	10-12	3	Biceps curl	Low pulley curl	Preacher curl

Rest period: 1 minute

Cool-down: Slow walking for 5 minutes followed by stretching

Workout tips

* Be sure to perform the sets for exercises 2 and 5 back to back and in the order listed.

Level 4   Workout 4

Total time: 55 minutes

Weeks: 3 and 4

Days of the week: Two nonconsecutive days

Warm-up: Easy jogging or rope skipping for 5 minutes followed by stretching

Lower-body exercises: 25 minutes

Number	Muscle group	Reps	Sets	Free weight	Pivot machine	Cam machine
1	Thighs	10-12	2*	Squat	Leg press	Horizontal leg press
2	Thighs	10-12	3	Lunge	Leg press	Horizontal leg press
3	Back of thigh	10-12	2*	Leg (knee) curl	Leg (knee) curl	Leg (knee) curl
4	Front of thigh	10-12	2*	Leg (knee) extension	Leg (knee) extension	Leg (knee) extension
5	Calf	10-12	2*	Standing heel raise	Seated heel raise	Machine standing heel raise
6	Abdomen	15-25	3	Sit up	Abdominal crunch	Abdominal crunch

Rest period: 1 minute

Cool-down: Slow walking for 5 minutes followed by stretching

Workout tips

* Be sure to perform the sets for exercises 1, 3, 4, and 5 back to back and in the order listed.

Level 4   Workout 5

Total time: 1 hour, 8 minutes

Weeks: 5 and 6

Days of the week: Two nonconsecutive days

Warm-up: Easy jogging or rope skipping for 5 minutes followed by stretching

Upper-body exercises: 38 minutes

Number	Muscle group	Reps	Sets	Free weight	Pivot machine	Cam machine
1	Chest	10-12	3	Bench press	Bench press	Chest press
2	Chest	10-12	3*	Dumbbell fly	Pec deck	Pec deck
3	Back	10-12	3	Bent-over row	Seated row	Seated row
4	Shoulder	10-12	3	Standing press	Seated press	Shoulder press
5	Back	10-12	3*	One-arm dumbbell row	Lat pulldown	Machine pullover
6	Back of arm	10-12	3	Dumbbell triceps extension	Triceps pushdown	Triceps extension
7	Front of arm	10-12	3	Biceps curl	Low pulley curl	Preacher curl

Rest period: 1 minute

Cool-down: Slow walking for 5 minutes followed by stretching

Workout tips

* Be sure to perform the sets for exercises 2 and 5 back to back and in the order listed.

Level 4   Workout 6

Total time: 1 hour, 2 minutes
Weeks: 5 and 6
Days of the week: Two nonconsecutive days
Warm-up: Easy jogging or rope skipping for 5 minutes followed by stretching
Lower-body exercises: 32 minutes

Number	Muscle group	Reps	Sets	Free weight	Pivot machine	Cam machine
1	Thighs	10-12	3*	Squat	Leg press	Horizontal leg press
2	Thighs	10-12	3	Lunge	Leg press	Horizontal leg press
3	Back of thigh	10-12	3*	Leg (knee) curl	Leg (knee) curl	Leg (knee) curl
4	Front of thigh	10-12	3*	Leg (knee) extension	Leg (knee) extension	Leg (knee) extension
5	Calf	10-12	3*	Standing heel raise	Seated heel raise	Machine standing heel raise
6	Abdomen	15-25	3	Sit-up	Abdominal crunch	Abdominal crunch

Rest period: 1 minute

Cool-down: Slow walking for 5 minutes followed by stretching

Workout tips

* Be sure to perform the sets for exercises 1, 3, 4, and 5 back to back and in the order listed.

Level 5   Workout 1

Total time: 1 hour, 13 minutes

Weeks: 1 and 2

Days of the week: Two nonconsecutive days

Warm-up: Easy jogging or rope skipping for 5 minutes followed by stretching

Upper-body exercises: 43 minutes

Number	Muscle group	Reps	Sets	Free weight	Pivot machine	Cam machine
1	Chest	10-12	3	Bench press	Bench press	Chest press
2	Chest*	10-12	3	Dumbbell fly	Pec deck	Pec deck
3	Back	10-12	3	Bent-over row	Seated row	Seated row
4	Back*	10-12	3	One-arm dumbbell row	Lat pulldown	Machine pullover
5	Shoulder	10-12	3	Standing press	Seated press	Shoulder press
6**	Shoulder*	10-12	1	Dumbbell lateral raise	Machine lateral raise	Machine lateral raise
7	Front of arm	10-12	3	Biceps curl	Low pulley curl	Preacher curl
8**	Front of arm*	10-12	1	Dumbbell biceps curl	Biceps curl	Biceps curl
9	Back of arm	10-12	3	Dumbbell triceps extension	Triceps pushdown	Triceps extension
10**	Back of arm*	10-12	1	Lying triceps extension	Triceps extension	Triceps extension

Rest period: 1 minute

Cool-down: Slow walking for 5 minutes followed by stretching

Workout tips

* Because this program contains two exercises in a row for the same muscle group, you may need to adjust the load that you are using across all sets of both exercises to complete the desired number of repetitions.

** If you just completed level 4, note the changes made in the order of the exercises and the addition of three new exercises (6, 8, and 10). Refer to chapter 5 to determine your starting loads for new exercises and chapter 10 to learn how to perform them correctly.

Level 5   Workout 2

Total time: 1 hour, 6 minutes

Weeks: 1 and 2

Days of the week: Two nonconsecutive days

Warm-up: Easy jogging or rope skipping for 5 minutes followed by stretching

Lower-body exercises: 36 minutes

Number	Muscle group	Reps	Sets	Free weight	Pivot machine	Cam machine
1	Thighs	10-12	3	Squat	Leg press	Horizontal leg press
2	Thighs*	10-12	3	Lunge	Leg press	Horizontal leg press
3**	Thighs*	10-12	1	Angled leg press	Leg press	Horizontal leg press
4	Back of thigh	10-12	3	Leg (knee) curl	Leg (knee) curl	Leg (knee) curl
5	Front of thigh	10-12	3	Leg (knee) extension	Leg (knee) extension	Leg (knee) extension
6	Calf	10-12	3	Standing heel raise	Seated heel raise	Machine standing heel raise
7**	Calf*	10-12	1	Seated heel raise	Standing heel raise	Seated heel raise
8	Abdomen	15-25	3	Sit-up	Abdominal crunch	Abdominal crunch

Rest period: 1 minute

Cool-down: Slow walking for 5 minutes followed by stretching

Workout tips

* Because this program contains several exercises in a row for the same muscle group, you may need to adjust the load that you are using across all sets of the exercises to complete the desired number of repetitions.

** If you just completed level 4, note the changes made in the order of the exercises and the addition of two new exercises (3 and 7). Refer to chapter 5 to determine your starting loads for new exercises and chapter 10 to learn how to perform them correctly.

Level 5   Workout 3

Total time: 1 hour, 19 minutes

Weeks: 3 and 4

Days of the week: Two nonconsecutive days

Warm-up: Easy jogging or rope skipping for 5 minutes followed by stretching

Upper-body exercises: 49 minutes

Number	Muscle group	Reps	Sets	Free weight	Pivot machine	Cam machine
1	Chest	10-12	3	Bench press	Bench press	Chest press
2	Chest*	10-12	3	Dumbbell fly	Pec deck	Pec deck
3	Back	10-12	3	Bent-over row	Seated row	Seated row
4	Back*	10-12	3	One-arm dumbbell row	Lat pulldown	Machine pullover
5	Shoulder	10-12	3	Standing press	Seated press	Shoulder press
6	Shoulder*	10-12	2	Dumbbell lateral raise	Machine lateral raise	Machine lateral raise
7	Front of arm	10-12	3	Biceps curl	Low pulley curl	Preacher curl
8	Front of arm*	10-12	2	Dumbbell biceps curl	Biceps curl	Biceps curl
9	Back of arm	10-12	3	Dumbbell triceps extension	Triceps pushdown	Triceps extension
10	Back of arm*	10-12	2	Lying triceps extension	Triceps extension	Triceps extension

Rest period: 1 minute

Cool-down: Slow walking for 5 minutes followed by stretching

Workout tips

* Because this program contains sequential exercises for the same muscle group, you may need to adjust the load that you are using across all sets of the exercises to complete the desired number of repetitions in back-to-back sets.

Level 5   Workout 4

Total time: 1 hour, 10 minutes

Weeks: 3 and 4

Days of the week: Two nonconsecutive days

Warm-up: Easy jogging or rope skipping for 5 minutes followed by stretching

Lower-body exercises: 40 minutes

Number	Muscle group	Reps	Sets	Free weight	Pivot machine	Cam machine
1	Thighs	10-12	3	Squat	Leg press	Horizontal leg press
2	Thighs*	10-12	3	Lunge	Leg press	Horizontal leg press
3	Thighs*	10-12	2	Angled leg press	Leg press	Horizontal leg press
4	Back of thigh	10-12	3	Leg (knee) curl	Leg (knee) curl	Leg (knee) curl
5	Front of thigh	10-12	3	Leg (knee) extension	Leg (knee) extension	Leg (knee) extension
6	Calf	10-12	3	Standing heel raise	Seated heel raise	Machine standing heel raise
7	Calf*	10-12	2	Seated heel raise	Standing heel raise	Seated heel raise
8	Abdomen	15-25	3	Sit-up	Abdominal crunch	Abdominal crunch

Rest period: 1 minute

Cool-down: Slow walking for 5 minutes followed by stretching

Workout tips

* Because this program contains sequential exercises for the same muscle group, you may need to adjust the load that you are using across all sets of the exercises to complete the desired number of repetitions in back-to-back sets.

Level 5 Workout 5

Total time: 1 hour, 24 minutes

Weeks: 5 and 6

Days of the week: Two nonconsecutive days

Warm-up: Easy jogging or rope skipping for 5 minutes followed by stretching

Upper-body exercises: 54 minutes

Number	Muscle group	Reps	Sets	Free weight	Pivot machine	Cam machine
1	Chest	10-12	3	Bench press	Bench press	Chest press
2	Chest*	10-12	3	Dumbbell fly	Pec deck	Pec deck
3	Back	10-12	3	Bent-over row	Seated row	Seated row
4	Back*	10-12	3	One-arm dumbbell row	Lat pulldown	Machine pullover
5	Shoulder	10-12	3	Standing press	Seated press	Shoulder press
6	Shoulder*	10-12	3	Dumbbell lateral raise	Machine lateral raise	Machine lateral raise
7	Front of arm	10-12	3	Biceps curl	Low pulley curl	Preacher curl
8	Front of arm*	10-12	3	Dumbbell biceps curl	Biceps curl	Biceps curl
9	Back of arm	10-12	3	Dumbbell triceps extension	Triceps pushdown	Triceps extension
10	Back of arm*	10-12	3	Lying triceps extension	Triceps extension	Triceps extension

Rest period: 1 minute

Cool-down: Slow walking for 5 minutes followed by stretching

Workout tips

* Because this program contains sequential exercises for the same muscle group, you may need to adjust the load that you are using across all sets of the exercises to complete the desired number of repetitions in three back-to-back sets.

Level 5   Workout 6

Total time: 1 hour, 13 minutes

Weeks: 5 and 6

Days of the week: Two nonconsecutive days

Warm-up: Easy jogging or rope skipping for 5 minutes followed by stretching

Lower-body exercises: 43 minutes

Number	Muscle group	Reps	Sets	Free weight	Pivot machine	Cam machine
1	Thighs	10-12	3	Squat	Leg press	Horizontal leg press
2	Thighs*	10-12	3	Lunge	Leg press	Horizontal leg press
3	Thighs*	10-12	3	Angled leg press	Leg press	Horizontal leg press
4	Back of thigh	10-12	3	Leg (knee) curl	Leg (knee) curl	Leg (knee) curl
5	Front of thigh	10-12	3	Leg (knee) extension	Leg (knee) extension	Leg (knee) extension
6	Calf	10-12	3	Standing heel raise	Seated heel raise	Machine standing heel raise
7	Calf*	10-12	3	Seated heel raise	Standing heel raise	Seated heel raise
8	Abdomen	15-25	3	Sit-up	Abdominal crunch	Abdominal crunch

Rest period: 1 minute

Cool-down: Slow walking for 5 minutes followed by stretching

Workout tips

* Because this program contains sequential exercises for the same muscle group, you may need to adjust the load that you are using across all sets of the exercises to complete the desired number of repetitions in three back-to-back sets.

Level 6   Workout 1

Total time: 1 hour, 24 minutes

Weeks: 1 and 2

Days of the week: Two nonconsecutive days

Warm-up: Easy jogging or rope skipping for 5 minutes followed by stretching

Upper-body exercises: 54 minutes

Number	Muscle group	Reps	Sets	Free weight	Pivot machine	Cam machine
1	Chest	10-12 8-10*	2 1*	Bench press	Bench press	Chest press
2	Chest	10-12	3	Dumbbell fly	Pec deck	Pec deck
3	Back	10-12	3	Bent-over row	Seated row	Seated row
4	Back	10-12	3	One-arm dumbbell row	Lat pulldown	Machine pullover
5	Shoulder	10-12 8-10*	2 1*	Standing press	Seated press	Shoulder press
6	Shoulder	10-12	3	Dumbbell lateral raise	Machine lateral raise	Machine lateral raise
7	Front of arm	10-12	3	Biceps curl	Low pulley curl	Preacher curl
8	Front of arm	10-12	3	Dumbbell biceps curl	Biceps curl	Biceps curl
9	Back of arm	10-12	3	Dumbbell triceps extension	Triceps pushdown	Triceps extension
10	Back of arm	10-12	3	Lying triceps extension	Triceps extension	Triceps extension

Rest period: 1 minute

Cool-down: Slow walking for 5 minutes followed by stretching

Workout tips

   * When you make the change to performing sets of 8 to 10 repetitions instead of 10 to 12 repetitions, a general guideline is to add 5 to 10 pounds to your upper-body exercises. At this point you only have to lift the heavier weight (and perform fewer repetitions) in the third of the three sets for exercises 1 and 5.

Level 6   Workout 2

Total time: 1 hour, 13 minutes

Weeks: 1 and 2

Days of the week: Two nonconsecutive days

Warm-up: Easy jogging or rope skipping for 5 minutes followed by stretching

Lower-body exercises: 43 minutes

Number	Muscle group	Reps	Sets	Free weight	Pivot machine	Cam machine
1	Thighs	10-12 8-10*	2 1*	Squat	Leg press	Horizontal leg press
2	Thighs	10-12 8-10*	2 1*	Lunge	Leg press	Horizontal leg press
3	Thighs	10-12	3	Angled leg press	Leg press	Horizontal leg press
4	Back of thigh	10-12	3	Leg (knee) curl	Leg (knee) curl	Leg (knee) curl
5	Front of thigh	10-12	3	Leg (knee) extension	Leg (knee) extension	Leg (knee) extension
6	Calf	10-12	3	Standing heel raise	Seated heel raise	Machine standing heel raise
7	Calf	10-12	3	Seated heel raise	Standing heel raise	Seated heel raise
8	Abdomen	15-25	3	Sit-up	Abdominal crunch	Abdominal crunch

Rest period: 1 minute

Cool-down: Slow walking for 5 minutes followed by stretching

Workout tips

* When you make the change to performing sets of 8 to 10 repetitions instead of 10 to 12 repetitions, a general guideline is to add 10 to 20 pounds to your lower-body exercises. At this point you only have to lift the heavier weight (and perform fewer repetitions) in the third of the three sets for exercises 1 and 2.

Level 6   Workout 3

Total time: 1 hour, 24 minutes

Weeks: 3 and 4

Days of the week: Two nonconsecutive days

Warm-up: Easy jogging or rope skipping for 5 minutes followed by stretching

Upper-body exercises: 54 minutes

Number	Muscle group	Reps	Sets	Free weight	Pivot machine	Cam machine
1	Chest	10-12 8-10*	1 2*	Bench press	Bench press	Chest press
2	Chest	10-12	3	Dumbbell fly	Pec deck	Pec deck
3	Back	10-12	3	Bent-over row	Seated row	Seated row
4	Back	10-12	3	One-arm dumbbell row	Lat pulldown	Machine pullover
5	Shoulder	10-12 8-10*	1 2*	Standing press	Seated press	Shoulder press
6	Shoulder	10-12	3	Dumbbell lateral raise	Machine lateral raise	Machine lateral raise
7	Front of arm	10-12	3	Biceps curl	Low pulley curl	Preacher curl
8	Front of arm	10-12	3	Dumbbell biceps curl	Biceps curl	Biceps curl
9	Back of arm	10-12	3	Dumbbell triceps extension	Triceps pushdown	Triceps extension
10	Back of arm	10-12	3	Lying triceps extension	Triceps extension	Triceps extension

Rest period: 1 minute

Cool-down: Slow walking for 5 minutes followed by stretching

Workout tips

   * In comparison to level 6, upper-body workout 1, this workout assigns a heavier load for the second set (in addition to the third set) of exercises 1 and 5, so you may need to adjust the load that you are using in the third set to complete 8 to 10 repetitions.

Level 6   Workout 4

Total time: 1 hour, 13 minutes

Weeks: 3 and 4

Days of the week: Two nonconsecutive days

Warm-up: Easy jogging or rope skipping for 5 minutes followed by stretching

Lower-body exercises: 43 minutes

Number	Muscle group	Reps	Sets	Free weight	Pivot machine	Cam machine
1	Thighs	10-12 8-10*	1 2*	Squat	Leg press	Horizontal leg press
2	Thighs	10-12 8-10*	1 2*	Lunge	Leg press	Horizontal leg press
3	Thighs	10-12	3	Angled leg press	Leg press	Horizontal leg press
4	Back of thigh	10-12	3	Leg (knee) curl	Leg (knee) curl	Leg (knee) curl
5	Front of thigh	10-12	3	Leg (knee) extension	Leg (knee) extension	Leg (knee) extension
6	Calf	10-12	3	Standing heel raise	Seated heel raise	Machine standing heel raise
7	Calf	10-12	3	Seated heel raise	Standing heel raise	Seated heel raise
8	Abdomen	15-25	3	Sit-up	Abdominal crunch	Abdominal crunch

Rest period: 1 minute

Cool-down: Slow walking for 5 minutes followed by stretching

Workout tips

* In comparison to level 6, lower-body workout 2, this workout assigns a heavier load for the second set (in addition to the third set) of exercises 1 and 2, so you may need to adjust the load that you are using in the third set to complete 8 to 10 repetitions.

Level 6   Workout 5

Total time: 1 hour, 27 minutes

Weeks: 5 and 6

Days of the week: Two nonconsecutive days

Warm-up: Easy jogging or rope skipping for 5 minutes followed by stretching

Upper-body exercises: 57 minutes

Number	Muscle group	Reps	Sets	Free weight	Pivot machine	Cam machine
1	Chest	10-12 8-10*	2 2*	Bench press	Bench press	Chest press
2	Chest	10-12	3	Dumbbell fly	Pec deck	Pec deck
3	Back	10-12	3	Bent-over row	Seated row	Seated row
4	Back	10-12	3	One-arm dumbbell row	Lat pulldown	Machine pullover
5	Shoulder	10-12 8-10*	2 2*	Standing press	Seated press	Shoulder press
6	Shoulder	10-12	3	Dumbbell lateral raise	Machine lateral raise	Machine lateral raise
7	Front of arm	10-12	3	Biceps curl	Low pulley curl	Preacher curl
8	Front of arm	10-12	3	Dumbbell biceps curl	Biceps curl	Biceps curl
9	Back of arm	10-12	3	Dumbbell triceps extension	Triceps pushdown	Triceps extension
10	Back of arm	10-12	3	Lying triceps extension	Triceps extension	Triceps extension

Rest period: 1 minute

Cool-down: Slow walking for 5 minutes followed by stretching

Workout tips

   * Because you are performing four sets of exercises 1 and 5, you may need to adjust the load that you are using in the third and fourth sets to complete 8 to 10 repetitions.

Level 6   Workout 6

Total time. 1 hour, 16 minutes

Weeks: 5 and 6

Days of the week: Two nonconsecutive days

Warm-up: Easy jogging or rope skipping for 5 minutes followed by stretching

Lower-body exercises: 46 minutes

Number	Muscle group	Reps	Sets	Free weight	Pivot machine	Cam machine
1	Thighs	10-12 8-10*	2 2*	Squat	Leg press	Horizontal leg press
2	Thighs	10-12 8-10*	2 2*	Lunge	Leg press	Horizontal leg press
3	Thighs	10-12	3	Angled leg prooo	Leg press	Horizontal leg press
4	Back of thigh	10-12	3	Leg (knee) curl	Leg (knee) curl	Leg (knee) curl
5	Front of thigh	10-12	3	Leg (knee) extension	Leg (knee) extension	Leg (knee) extension
6	Calf	10-12	3	Standing heel raise	Seated heel raise	Machine standing heel raise
7	Calf	10-12	3	Seated heel raise	Standing heel raise	Seated heel raise
8	Abdomen	15-25	3	Sit-up	Abdominal crunch	Abdominal crunch

Rest period: 1 minute

Cool-down: Slow walking for 5 minutes followed by stretching

Workout tips

* Because you are performing four sets of exercises 1 and 2, you may need to adjust the load that you are using in the third and fourth sets to complete 8 to 10 repetitions.

9

Strength Training

This type of weight training program focuses on making the trained muscles stronger so that they will be able to exert more force or effort. Because this program requires the lifting of heavier loads, only those who have been weight training should follow this program (especially beginning with level 2).

Training Goal Highlights

Level 1

- The strength-training program begins with three workouts per week that consist of one set of 12 to 15 reps for seven exercises. The program includes an exercise for each major muscle group: chest, back, shoulders, front of the upper arm (biceps), back of the upper arm (triceps), thighs, and abdomen.
- The number of sets increases from one to two in the third week, and by the fifth week, you perform those two sets back to back.

Level 2

- Weeks 1 and 2 decrease the number of reps to 10 to 12 in the second set (only) of all exercises. Be sure to increase the weight slightly in the second set (see chapter 5).
- Weeks 3 and 4 require that you perform both sets with a slightly heavier weight for 10 to 12 reps in all exercises.

- Weeks 5 and 6 again decrease the number of reps (which means that you need to add weight) to 8 to 10 in the second set (only) of the three major exercises (those that train the chest, shoulders, and thighs).

Level 3

- A major change in level 3 is that you will be completing four workouts each week; your program includes two upper-body and two lower-body training days. Because of the increase in the number of weekly workouts, weeks 1 and 2 will require only one set of 10 to 12 reps in the two new upper-body exercises and the four new lower-body exercises. (An exception is that you will do 8 to 10 reps in the new thigh exercise.) The upper-body exercises include two each for the chest and back and one each for the shoulders, front of the upper arm (biceps), and back of the upper arm (triceps). The lower-body exercises include two for the thighs and one each for the back of the thigh (hamstrings), the front of the thigh (quadriceps), the calves, and the abdomen. Chapter 5 will help you determine the loads for your new exercises.
- Weeks 3 through 6 gradually increase the number of sets so that you will be performing three back-to-back sets in the two major upper-body exercises (a chest exercise and the shoulder exercise) and in the two major lower-body exercises (both thigh exercises). The other exercises require only two sets.

Level 4

- Weeks 1 and 2 add more sets (now you will be doing three) in the exercises that you were performing only two sets of at the end of level 3.
- Weeks 3 and 4 add more sets (now you will be doing four) in the two major upper-body exercises and the first lower-body thigh exercise. These three exercises are termed the *core exercises* because they are the important exercises that you will use to build strength during the rest of level 4 and on through level 6.
- At week 5, the strength-training program makes another increase in training intensity. Depending on the exercise, the program now has different repetition goals: 6 to 8 reps for the core exercises and 8 to 10 or 10 to 12 reps for all others. In addition, you will begin performing weight training exercises as part of your warm-up. Follow the warm-up procedure outlined in the warm-up section of each strength-training workout (those sets are not counted in the number of sets that the program requires you to complete).
- Remember to increase the weight slightly for the core exercises when you begin performing 6 to 8 reps per set.

Level 5

- Weeks 1 and 2 add one set (now you will be doing four) to the three core exercises.
- For weeks 3 and 4, the core exercises now require you to perform only 4 to 6 reps, but you use a slightly heavier weight. Because of this increase, you need to complete only three sets per core exercise.
- Weeks 5 and 6 gradually return you to four sets in each core exercise.

Level 6

- For weeks 1 and 2, the core exercises now require you to perform only 2 to 4 reps, but you need to add weight again. Because of this change, you need to complete only three sets per core exercise.
- Weeks 3 through 6 gradually add sets to the core exercises.
- By the end of week 6 of level 6, you will be performing five sets of 2 to 4 repetitions in your core exercises and three sets of 10 to 12 repetitions in five upper-body and five lower body exercises during four workouts per week!

Level 1   Workout 1

Total time: 44 minutes

Weeks: 1 and 2

Days of the week: Three nonconsecutive days*

Warm-up: Easy jogging or rope skipping for 5 minutes followed by stretching

Exercises: 14 minutes

Number	Muscle group	Reps	Sets	Free weight	Pivot machine	Cam machine
1	Chest	12-15	1	Bench press	Bench press	Chest press
2	Back	12-15	1	Bent-over row	Lat pulldown	Seated row
3	Shoulders	12-15	1	Standing press	Seated press	Shoulder press
4	Front of arm	12-15	1	Biceps curl	Low pulley curl	Preacher curl
5	Back of arm	12-15	1	Lying triceps extension	Triceps pushdown	Triceps extension
6	Thighs	12-15	1	Squat	Leg press	Horizontal leg press
7	Abdomen	12-15	1	Sit-up	Abdominal crunch	Abdominal crunch

Rest period: 30 seconds**

Cool-down: Slow walking for 5 minutes followed by stretching

Workout tips

* Be sure to spread out your weight training sessions throughout the week; you need at least one rest day (but no more than three) between workouts. A common three-days-per-week program is Monday, Wednesday, and Friday or Tuesday, Thursday, and one weekend day.

** You may want to rest for up to 60 seconds between exercises for your first or second week of training, or both.

Level 1   Workout 2

Total time: 51 minutes

Weeks: 3 and 4

Days of the week: Three nonconsecutive days

Warm-up: Easy jogging or rope skipping for 5 minutes followed by stretching

Exercises: 21 minutes

Number	Muscle group	Reps	Sets*	Free weight	Pivot machine	Cam machine
1	Chest	12-15	2	Bench press	Bench press	Chest press
2	Back	12-15	2	Bent-over row	Lat pulldown	Seated row
3	Shoulders	12-15	2	Standing press	Seated press	Shoulder press
4	Front of arm	12-15	2	Biceps curl	Low pulley curl	Preacher curl
5	Back of arm	12-15	2	Lying triceps extension	Triceps pushdown	Triceps extension
6	Thighs	12-15	2	Squat	Leg press	Horizontal leg press
7	Abdomen	12-15	2	Sit-up	Abdominal crunch	Abdominal crunch

Rest period: 30 seconds

Cool-down: Slow walking for 5 minutes followed by stretching

Workout tips

* Complete one set of each exercise and then start over and perform the second set of each exercise (as opposed to doing two sets of each exercise back to back).

Level 1   Workout 3

Total time: 51 minutes

Weeks: 5 and 6

Days of the week: Three nonconsecutive days

Warm-up: Easy jogging or rope skipping for 5 minutes followed by stretching

Exercises: 21 minutes

Number	Muscle group	Reps	Sets*	Free weight	Pivot machine	Cam machine
1	Chest	12-15	2	Bench press	Bench press	Chest press
2	Back	12-15	2	Bent-over row	Lat pulldown	Seated row
3	Shoulders	12-15	2	Standing press	Seated press	Shoulder press
4	Front of arm	12-15	2	Biceps curl	Low pulley curl	Preacher curl
5	Back of arm	12-15	2	Lying triceps extension	Triceps pushdown	Triceps extension
6	Thighs	12-15	2	Squat	Leg press	Horizontal leg press
7	Abdomen	12-15	2	Sit-up	Abdominal crunch	Abdominal crunch

Rest period: 30 seconds

Cool-down: Slow walking for 5 minutes followed by stretching

Workout tips

* At this point you should be able to perform the required two sets back to back.

Level 2   Workout 1

Total time: 53 minutes

Weeks: 1 and 2

Days of the week: Three nonconsecutive days

Warm-up: Easy jogging or rope skipping for 5 minutes followed by stretching

Exercises: 23 minutes

Number	Muscle group	Reps	Sets	Free weight	Pivot machine	Cam machine
1	Chest	12-15 10-12*	1 1	Bench press	Bench press	Chest press
2	Back	12-15 10-12*	1 1	Bent-over row	Lat pulldown	Seated row
3	Shoulders	12-15 10-12*	1 1	Standing press	Seated press	Shoulder press
4	Front of arm	12-15 10-12*	1 1	Biceps curl	Low pulley curl	Preacher curl
5	Back of arm	12-15 10-12*	1 1	Lying triceps extension	Triceps pushdown	Triceps extension
6	Thighs	12-15 10-12*	1 1	Squat	Leg press	Horizontal leg press
7	Abdomen	15-25**	2	Sit-up	Abdominal crunch	Abdominal crunch

Rest period: 1 minute after sets of 10 to 12 repetitions***; 30 seconds after sets of 12 to 15 repetitions

Cool-down: Slow walking for 5 minutes followed by stretching

Workout tips

   * When you make the change to performing sets of 10 to 12 repetitions instead of 12 to 15 repetitions, a general guideline is to add 5 to 10 pounds to your upper-body exercises and 10 to 20 pounds to your lower-body exercises. At this point you have to lift the heavier weight (and perform fewer repetitions) only in the second of the two sets.

  ** You are now doing sets of 15 to 25 reps for your abdominal exercise.

 *** The rest period after these heavier sets is longer (60 seconds versus 30 seconds).

Level 2   Workout 2

Total time: 55 minutes

Weeks: 3 and 4

Days of the week: Three nonconsecutive days

Warm-up: Easy jogging or rope skipping for 5 minutes followed by stretching

Exercises: 25 minutes

Number	Muscle group	Reps	Sets*	Free weight	Pivot machine	Cam machine
1	Chest	10-12	2	Bench press	Bench press	Chest press
2	Back	10-12	2	Bent-over row	Lat pulldown	Seated row
3	Shoulders	10-12	2	Standing press	Seated press	Shoulder press
4	Front of arm	10-12	2	Biceps curl	Low pulley curl	Preacher curl
5	Back of arm	10-12	2	Lying triceps extension	Triceps pushdown	Triceps extension
6	Thighs	10-12	2	Squat	Leg press	Horizontal leg press
7	Abdomen	15-25	2	Sit-up	Abdominal crunch	Abdominal crunch

Rest period: 1 minute

Cool-down: Slow walking for 5 minutes followed by stretching

Workout tips

* As you begin performing both sets with the heavier load (for fewer repetitions), you may have to decrease the load slightly in the second set to complete both sets.

Level 2   Workout 3

Total time: 55 minutes

Weeks: 5 and 6

Days of the week: Three nonconsecutive days

Warm-up: Easy jogging or rope skipping for 5 minutes followed by stretching

Exercises: 25 minutes

Number	Muscle group	Reps	Sets	Free weight	Pivot machine	Cam machine
1	Chest	10-12 8-10*	1 1	Bench press	Bench press	Chest press
2	Back	10-12	2	Bent-over row	Lat pulldown	Seated row
3	Shoulders	10-12 8-10*	1 1	Standing press	Seated press	Shoulder press
4	Front of arm	10-12	2	Biceps curl	Low pulley curl	Preacher curl
5	Back of arm	10-12	2	Lying triceps extension	Triceps pushdown	Triceps extension
6	Thighs	10-12 8-10*	1 1	Squat	Leg press	Horizontal leg press
7	Abdomen	15-25	2	Sit-up	Abdominal crunch	Abdominal crunch

Rest period: 1 minute

Cool-down: Slow walking for 5 minutes followed by stretching

Workout tips

* When you make the change to performing sets of 8 to 10 repetitions instead of 10 to 12 repetitions, a general guideline is to add 5 to 10 pounds to your upper-body exercises and 10 to 20 pounds to your lower-body exercises. At this point you have to lift the heavier weight (and perform fewer repetitions) only in the second of the two sets for exercises 1, 3, and 6.

Level 3   Workout 1

Total time: 51 minutes

Weeks: 1 and 2

Days of the week: Two nonconsecutive days*

Warm-up: Easy jogging or rope skipping for 5 minutes followed by stretching

Upper-body exercises: 21 minutes

Number	Muscle group	Reps	Sets	Free weight	Pivot machine	Cam machine
1	Chest	8-10	2**	Bench press	Bench press	Chest press
2***	Chest	10-12	1	Dumbbell fly	Pec deck	Pec deck
3	Back	10-12	2	Bent-over row	Lat pulldown	Seated row
4	Shoulders	8-10	2**	Standing press	Seated press	Shoulder press
5***	Back	10-12	1	One-arm dumbbell row	Seated row	Lat pulldown
6	Back of arm	10-12	2	Lying triceps extension	Triceps pushdown	Triceps extension
7	Front of arm	10-12	2	Biceps curl	Low pulley curl	Preacher curl

Rest period: 1 minute

Cool-down: Slow walking for 5 minutes followed by stretching

Workout tips

   * When you make the change to four workouts per week, you will perform upper-body and lower-body workouts separately, allowing you to add new exercises and still complete your workouts in about the same amount of time. A common program schedules upper-body exercises on Mondays and Thursdays and lower-body exercises on Tuesdays and Fridays.

  ** As you begin performing both sets with the heavier load (for fewer repetitions), you may have to decrease the load slightly in the second set to complete both sets in exercises 1 and 4.

 *** Refer to chapter 5 to determine your starting loads for new exercises and chapter 10 to learn how to perform them correctly.

Level 3   Workout 2

Total time: 44 minutes

Weeks: 1 and 2

Days of the week: Two nonconsecutive days*

Warm-up: Easy jogging or rope skipping for 5 minutes followed by stretching

Lower-body exercises: 14 minutes

Number	Muscle group	Reps	Sets	Free weight	Pivot machine	Cam machine
1	Thighs	8-10	2**	Squat	Leg press	Horizontal leg press
2***	Thighs	8-10	1	Angled leg press	Leg press	Horizontal leg press
3***	Back of thigh	10-12	1	Leg (knee) curl	Leg (knee) curl	Leg (knee) curl
4***	Front of thigh	10-12	1	Leg (knee) extension	Leg (knee) extension	Leg (knee) extension
5***	Calf	10-12	1	Standing heel raise	Seated heel raise	Machine standing heel raise
6	Abdomen	15-25	2	Sit-up	Abdominal crunch	Abdominal crunch

Rest period: 1 minute

Cool down: Slow walking for 5 minutes followed by stretching

Workout tips

* When you make the change to four workouts per week, you will perform upper-body and lower-body workouts separately, allowing you to add new exercises and still complete your workouts in about the same amount of time. A common program schedules upper-body exercises on Mondays and Thursdays and lower-body exercises on Tuesdays and Fridays.

** As you begin performing both sets with the heavier load (for fewer repetitions), you may have to decrease the load slightly in the second set to complete both sets in exercise 1.

*** Refer to chapter 5 to determine your starting loads for new exercises and chapter 10 to learn how to perform them correctly.

Level 3 Workout 3

Total time: 55 minutes

Weeks: 3 and 4

Days of the week: Two nonconsecutive days

Warm-up: Easy jogging or rope skipping for 5 minutes followed by stretching

Upper-body exercises: 25 minutes

Number	Muscle group	Reps	Sets	Free weight	Pivot machine	Cam machine
1	Chest	8-10	2	Bench press	Bench press	Chest press
2	Chest	10-12	2*	Dumbbell fly	Pec deck	Pec deck
3	Back	10-12	2	Bent-over row	Lat pulldown	Seated row
4	Shoulders	8-10	2	Standing press	Seated press	Shoulder press
5	Back	10-12	2*	One-arm dumbbell row	Seated row	Lat pulldown
6	Back of arm	10-12	2	Lying triceps extension	Triceps pushdown	Triceps extension
7	Front of arm	10-12	2	Biceps curl	Low pulley curl	Preacher curl

Rest period: 1 minute

Cool-down: Slow walking for 5 minutes followed by stretching

Workout tips

   * You may need to readjust the loads that you are using in your new exercises to complete two back-to-back sets.

Level 3   Workout 4

Total time: 51 minutes

Weeks: 3 and 4

Days of the week: Two nonconsecutive days

Warm-up: Easy jogging or rope skipping for 5 minutes followed by stretching

Lower-body exercises: 21 minutes

Number	Muscle group	Reps	Sets	Free weight	Pivot machine	Cam machine
1	Thighs	8-10	2	Squat	Leg press	Horizontal leg press
2	Thighs	8-10	2*	Angled leg press	Leg press	Horizontal leg press
3	Back of thigh	10-12	2*	Leg (knee) curl	Leg (knee) curl	Leg (knee) curl
4	Front of thigh	10-12	2*	Leg (knee) extension	Leg (knee) extension	Leg (knee) extension
5	Calf	10-12	2*	Standing heel raise	Seated heel raise	Machine standing heel raise
6	Abdomen	15-25	2	Sit-up	Abdominal crunch	Abdominal crunch

Rest period: 1 minute

Cool-down: Slow walking for 5 minutes followed by stretching

Workout tips

  * You may need to readjust the loads that you are using in your new exercises to complete two back-to-back sets.

Level 3   Workout 5

Total time: 58 minutes

Weeks: 5 and 6

Days of the week: Two nonconsecutive days

Warm-up: Easy jogging or rope skipping for 5 minutes followed by stretching

Upper-body exercises: 28 minutes

Number	Muscle group	Reps	Sets	Free weight	Pivot machine	Cam machine
1	Chest	8-10	3*	Bench press	Bench press	Chest press
2	Chest	10-12	2	Dumbbell fly	Pec deck	Pec deck
3	Back	10-12	2	Bent-over row	Lat pulldown	Seated row
4	Shoulders	8-10	3*	Standing press	Seated press	Shoulder press
5	Back	10-12	2	One-arm dumbbell row	Seated row	Lat pulldown
6	Back of arm	10-12	2	Lying triceps extension	Triceps pushdown	Triceps extension
7	Front of arm	10-12	2	Biceps curl	Low pulley curl	Preacher curl

Rest period: 1 minute

Cool-down: Slow walking for 5 minutes followed by stretching

Workout tips

* To increase the difficulty of exercises 1 and 4, keep readjusting the load to perform 8 reps per set instead of 10. To do this, apply the two-for-two rule when you reach 10 reps in the last set for two consecutive workouts.

Level 3   Workout 6

Total time: 54 minutes

Weeks: 5 and 6

Days of the week: Two nonconsecutive days

Warm-up: Easy jogging or rope skipping for 5 minutes followed by stretching

Lower-body exercises: 24 minutes

Number	Muscle group	Reps	Sets	Free weight	Pivot machine	Cam machine
1	Thighs	8-10	3*	Squat	Leg press	Horizontal leg press
2	Thighs	8-10	3*	Angled leg press	Leg press	Horizontal leg press
3	Back of thigh	10-12	2	Leg (knee) curl	Leg (knee) curl	Leg (knee) curl
4	Front of thigh	10-12	2	Leg (knee) extension	Leg (knee) extension	Leg (knee) extension
5	Calf	10-12	2	Standing heel raise	Seated heel raise	Machine standing heel raise
6	Abdomen	15-25	3	Sit-up	Abdominal crunch	Abdominal crunch

Rest period: 1 minute

Cool-down: Slow walking for 5 minutes followed by stretching

Workout tips

* To increase the difficulty of exercises 1 and 2, keep readjusting the load to perform 8 reps per set instead of 10. To do this, apply the two-for-two rule when you reach 10 reps in the last set for two consecutive workouts.

Level 4   Workout 1

Total time: 1 hour, 17 minutes

Weeks: 1 and 2

Days of the week: Two nonconsecutive days

Warm-up: Easy jogging or rope skipping for 5 minutes followed by stretching

Upper-body exercises: 37 minutes

Number	Muscle group	Reps	Sets*	Free weight	Pivot machine	Cam machine
1	Chest	8-10	3	Bench press**	Bench press	Chest press
2	Chest	10-12	3	Dumbbell fly	Pec deck	Pec deck
3	Back	10-12	3	Bent-over row	Lat pulldown	Seated row
4	Shoulders	8-10	3	Standing press**	Seated Press	Shoulder Press
5	Back	10-12	3	One-arm dumbbell row	Seated row	Lat pulldown
6	Back of arm	10-12	3	Lying triceps extension	Triceps pushdown	Triceps extension
7	Front of arm	10-12	3	Biceps curl	Low pulley curl	Preacher curl

Rest period: 1 minute

Cool-down: Slow walking for 5 minutes followed by stretching

Workout tips

* You may need to readjust the loads to complete three back-to-back sets.

** As the loads become heavier, remember to use a spotter, especially for the free-weight version of exercises 1 and 4.

Level 4   Workout 2

Total time: 1 hour, 2 minutes

Weeks: 1 and 2

Days of the week: Two nonconsecutive days

Warm-up: Easy jogging or rope skipping for 5 minutes followed by stretching

Lower-body exercises: 32 minutes

Number	Muscle group	Reps	Sets*	Free weight	Pivot machine	Cam machine
1	Thighs	8-10	3	Squat**	Leg press	Horizontal leg press
2	Thighs	8-10	3	Angled leg press**	Leg press	Horizontal leg press
3	Back of thigh	10-12	3	Leg (knee) curl	Leg (knee) curl	Leg (knee) curl
4	Front of thigh	10-12	3	Leg (knee) extension	Leg (knee) extension	Leg (knee) extension
5	Calf	10-12	3	Standing heel raise	Seated heel raise	Machine standing heel raise
6	Abdomen	15-25	3	Sit-up	Abdominal crunch	Abdominal crunch

Rest period: 1 minute

Cool-down: Slow walking for 5 minutes followed by stretching

Workout tips

  * You may need to readjust the loads to complete three back-to-back sets.

  ** As the loads become heavier, remember to use a spotter, especially for the free-weight version of exercises 1 and 2.

Level 4   Workout 3

Total time: 1 hour, 10 minutes

Weeks: 3 and 4

Days of the week: Two nonconsecutive days

Warm-up: Easy jogging or rope skipping for 5 minutes followed by stretching

Upper-body exercises: 40 minutes

Number	Muscle group	Reps	Sets	Free weight	Pivot machine	Cam machine
1	Chest	8-10	4*	Bench press	Bench press	Chest press
2	Chest	10-12	3	Dumbbell fly	Pec deck	Pec deck
3	Back	10-12	3	Bent-over row	Lat pulldown	Seated row
4	Shoulders	8-10	4*	Standing press	Seated press	Shoulder press
5	Back	10-12	3	One-arm dumbbell row	Seated row	Lat pulldown
6	Back of arm	10-12	3	Lying triceps extension	Triceps pushdown	Triceps extension
7	Front of arm	10-12	3	Biceps curl	Low pulley curl	Preacher curl

Rest period: 1 minute

Cool-down: Slow walking for 5 minutes followed by stretching

Workout tips

   * As you begin performing four sets in exercises 1 and 4, you may have to decrease the load by 5 pounds to complete all four sets.

Level 4   Workout 4

Total time: 1 hour, 3 minutes

Weeks: 3 and 4

Days of the week: Two nonconsecutive days

Warm-up: Easy jogging or rope skipping for 5 minutes followed by stretching

Lower-body exercises: 33 minutes

Number	Muscle group	Reps	Sets	Free weight	Pivot machine	Cam machine
1	Thighs	8-10	4*	Squat	Leg press	Horizontal leg press
2	Thighs	8-10	3	Angled leg press	Leg press	Horizontal leg press
3	Back of thigh	10-12	3	Leg (knee) curl	Leg (knee) curl	Leg (knee) curl
4	Front of thigh	10-12	3	Leg (knee) extension	Leg (knee) extension	Leg (knee) extension
5	Calf	10-12	3	Standing heel raise	Seated heel raise	Machine standing heel raise
6	Abdomen	15-25	3	Sit-up	Abdominal crunch	Abdominal crunch

Rest period: 1 minute

Cool-down: Slow walking for 5 minutes followed by stretching

Workout tips

* As you begin performing four sets in exercise 1, you may have to decrease the load by 10 pounds to complete all four sets.

Level 4 Workout 5

Total time: 1 hour, 16 minutes

Weeks: 5 and 6

Days of the week: Two nonconsecutive days

Warm-up: Easy jogging or rope skipping for 5 minutes followed by stretching. Before performing your first set of exercises 1 and 4, do one warm-up set of 8 to 10 repetitions with half to three-quarters of the load that you typically use for that exercise. Rest 1 to 2 minutes before starting your scheduled sets.

Upper-body exercises: 46 minutes

Number	Muscle group	Reps	Sets	Free weight	Pivot machine	Cam machine
1	Chest	6-8*	3	Bench press	Bench press	Chest press
2	Chest	10-12	3	Dumbbell fly	Pec deck	Pec deck
3	Back	10-12	3	Bent-over row	Lat pulldown	Seated row
4	Shoulders	6-8*	3	Standing press	Seated press	Shoulder press
5	Back	10-12	3	One-arm dumbbell row	Seated row	Lat pulldown
6	Back of arm	10-12	3	Lying triceps extension	Triceps pushdown	Triceps extension
7	Front of arm	10-12	3	Biceps curl	Low pulley curl	Preacher curl

Rest period: 2 minutes for exercises 1 and 4**; 1 minute for all others

Cool-down: Slow walking for 5 minutes followed by stretching

Workout tips

* In exercises 1 and 4 you will perform 6 to 8 reps. To do this, add 5 to 10 pounds to the loads from the level 4, workout 3 or consult chapter 5 for a more specific method of determining new loads.

** Notice that the heavier sets of 6 to 8 repetitions require more rest between sets and a spotter for the free-weight version of exercises 1 and 4.

Level 4   Workout 6

Total time: 1 hour, 6 minutes

Weeks: 5 and 6

Days of the week: Two nonconsecutive days

Warm-up: Easy jogging or rope skipping for 5 minutes followed by stretching. Before performing your first set of exercise 1, do one warm-up set of 8 to 10 repetitions with half to three-quarters of the load that you typically use for that exercise. Rest 1 to 2 minutes before starting your scheduled sets.

Lower-body exercises: 36 minutes

Number	Muscle group	Reps	Sets	Free weight	Pivot machine	Cam machine
1	Thighs	6-8*	3	Squat	Leg press	Horizontal leg press
2	Thighs	8-10	3	Angled leg press	Leg press	Horizontal leg press
3	Back of thigh	10-12	3	Leg (knee) curl	Leg (knee) curl	Leg (knee) curl
4	Front of thigh	10-12	3	Leg (knee) extension	Leg (knee) extension	Leg (knee) extension
5	Calf	10-12	3	Standing heel raise	Seated heel raise	Machine standing heel raise
6	Abdomen	15-25	3	Sit-up	Abdominal crunch	Abdominal crunch

Rest period: 2 minutes for exercise 1**; 1 minute for all others

Cool-down: Slow walking for 5 minutes followed by stretching

Workout tips

* In exercise 1 you will perform 6 to 8 reps. To do this, add 10 to 20 pounds to the loads from the level 4, workout 4 or consult chapter 5 for a more specific method of determining new loads.

** Notice that the heavier sets of 6 to 8 repetitions require more rest between sets and a spotter for the free-weight version of exercises 1 and 2.

Level 5   Workout 1

Total time: 1 hour, 21 minutes

Weeks: 1 and 2

Days of the week: Two nonconsecutive days

Warm-up: Easy jogging or rope skipping for 5 minutes followed by stretching. Before performing your first set of exercises 1 and 4, do one warm-up set of 8 to 10 repetitions with half to three-quarters of the load that you typically use for that exercise. Rest 1 to 2 minutes before starting your scheduled sets.

Upper-body exercises: 51 minutes

Number	Muscle group	Reps	Sets	Free weight	Pivot machine	Cam machine
1	Chest	6-8	4*	Bench press	Bench press	Chest press
2	Chest	10-12	3	Dumbbell fly	Pec deck	Pec deck
3	Back	10-12	3	Bent-over row	Lat pulldown	Seated row
4	Shoulders	6-8	4*	Standing press	Seated press	Shoulder press
5	Back	10-12	3	One-arm dumbbell row	Seated row	Lat pulldown
6	Back of arm	10-12	3	Lying triceps extension	Triceps pushdown	Triceps extension
7	Front of arm	10-12	3	Biceps curl	Low pulley curl	Preacher curl

Rest period: 2 minutes for exercises 1 and 4; 1 minute for all others

Cool-down: Slow walking for 5 minutes followed by stretching

Workout tips

* As you begin performing four sets in exercises 1 and 4, you may have to decrease the load by 5 pounds to complete all four sets.

Level 5   Workout 2

Total time: 1 hour, 8 minutes

Weeks: 1 and 2

Days of the week: Two nonconsecutive days

Warm-up: Easy jogging or rope skipping for 5 minutes followed by stretching. Before performing your first set of exercise 1, do one warm-up set of 8 to 10 repetitions with half to three-quarters of the load that you typically use for that exercise. Rest 1 to 2 minutes before starting your scheduled sets.

Lower-body exercises: 38 minutes

Number	Muscle group	Reps	Sets	Free weight	Pivot machine	Cam machine
1	Thighs	6-8	4*	Squat	Leg press	Horizontal leg press
2	Thighs	8-10	3	Angled leg press	Leg press	Horizontal leg press
3	Back of thigh	10-12	3	Leg (knee) curl	Leg (knee) curl	Leg (knee) curl
4	Front of thigh	10-12	3	Leg (knee) extension	Leg (knee) extension	Leg (knee) extension
5	Calf	10-12	3	Standing heel raise	Seated heel raise	Machine standing heel raise
6	Abdomen	15-25	3	Sit-up	Abdominal crunch	Abdominal crunch

Rest period: 2 minutes for exercise 1; 1 minute for all others

Cool-down: Slow walking for 5 minutes followed by stretching

Workout tips

* As you begin performing four sets in exercise 1, you may have to decrease the load by 10 pounds to complete all four sets.

Level 5 Workout 3

Total time: 1 hour, 30 minutes

Weeks: 3 and 4

Days of the week: Two nonconsecutive days

Warm-up: Easy jogging or rope skipping for 5 minutes followed by stretching. Before performing your first set of exercises 1 and 4, do two warm-up sets of 8 to 10 and 4 to 6 repetitions with half and three-quarters, respectively, of the load that you typically use for that exercise. Rest 1 to 3 minutes before starting your scheduled sets.

Upper-body exercises: 1 hour

Number	Muscle group	Reps	Sets	Free weight	Pivot machine	Cam machine
1	Chest	4-6*	3	Bench press	Bench press	Chest press
2	Chest	10-12	3	Dumbbell fly	Pec deck	Pec deck
3	Back	10-12	3	Bent-over row	Lat pulldown	Seated row
4	Shoulders	4-6*	3	Standing press	Seated press	Shoulder press
5	Back	10-12	3	One-arm dumbbell row	Seated row	Lat pulldown
6	Back of arm	10-12	3	Lying triceps extension	Triceps pushdown	Triceps extension
7	Front of arm	10-12	3	Biceps curl	Low pulley curl	Preacher curl

Rest period: 3 minutes for exercises 1 and 4**; 1 minute for all others

Cool-down: Slow walking for 5 minutes followed by stretching

Workout tips

* In exercises 1 and 4 you will perform 4 to 6 reps. To do this, add 5 to 10 pounds to the loads from the level 5, workout 1 or consult chapter 5 for a more specific method for determining new loads.

** Notice that the heavier sets of 4 to 6 repetitions require more rest between sets and a spotter for the free-weight version of exercises 1 and 4.

Level 5   Workout 4

Total time: 1 hour, 12 minutes

Weeks: 3 and 4

Days of the week: Two nonconsecutive days

Warm-up: Easy jogging or rope skipping for 5 minutes followed by stretching. Before performing your first set of exercise 1, do two warm-up sets of 8 to 10 and 4 to 6 repetitions with half and three-quarters, respectively, of the load that you typically use for that exercise. Rest 1 to 3 minutes before starting your scheduled sets.

Lower-body exercises: 42 minutes

Number	Muscle group	Reps	Sets	Free weight	Pivot machine	Cam machine
1	Thighs	4-6*	3	Squat	Leg press	Horizontal leg press
2	Thighs	8-10	3	Angled leg press	Leg press	Horizontal leg press
3	Back of thigh	10-12	3	Leg (knee) curl	Leg (knee) curl	Leg (knee) curl
4	Front of thigh	10-12	3	Leg (knee) extension	Leg (knee) extension	Leg (knee) extension
5	Calf	10-12	3	Standing heel raise	Seated heel raise	Machine standing heel raise
6	Abdomen	15-25	3	Sit-up	Abdominal crunch	Abdominal crunch

Rest period: 3 minutes for exercise 1**; 1 minute for all others

Cool-down: Slow walking for 5 minutes followed by stretching

Workout tips

* In exercise 1 you will perform 4 to 6 reps. To do this, add 10 to 20 pounds to the loads from the level 5, workout 2 or consult chapter 5 for a more specific method for determining new loads.

** Notice that the heavier sets of 4 to 6 repetitions require more rest between sets and a spotter for the free-weight version of exercises 1 and 2.

Level 5   Workout 5

Total time: 1 hour, 34 minutes

Weeks: 5 and 6

Days of the week: Two nonconsecutive days

Warm-up: Easy jogging or rope skipping for 5 minutes followed by stretching. Before performing your first set of exercises 1 and 4, do two warm-up sets of 8 to 10 and 4 to 6 repetitions with half and three-quarters, respectively, of the load that you typically use for that exercise. Rest 1 to 3 minutes before starting your scheduled sets.

Upper-body exercises: 1 hour, 4 minutes

Number	Muscle group	Reps	Sets	Free weight	Pivot machine	Cam machine
1	Chest	4-6	4*	Bench press	Bench press	Chest press
2	Chest	10-12	3	Dumbbell fly	Pec deck	Pec deck
3	Back	10-12	3	Bent-over row	Lat pulldown	Seated row
4	Shoulders	4-6	4*	Standing press	Seated press	Shoulder press
5	Back	10-12	3	One-arm dumbbell row	Seated row	Lat pulldown
6	Back of arm	10-12	3	Lying triceps extension	Triceps pushdown	Triceps extension
7	Front of arm	10-12	3	Biceps curl	Low pulley curl	Preacher curl

Rest period: 3 minutes for exercises 1 and 4; 1 minute for all others

Cool-down: Slow walking for 5 minutes followed by stretching

Workout tips

   * As you begin performing four sets in exercises 1 and 4, you may have to decrease the load by 5 pounds to complete all four sets.

Level 5   Workout 6

Total time: 1 hour, 15 minutes

Weeks: 5 and 6

Days of the week: Two nonconsecutive days

Warm-up: Easy jogging or rope skipping for 5 minutes followed by stretching. Before performing your first set of exercise 1, do two warm-up sets of 8 to 10 and 4 to 6 repetitions with half and three-quarters, respectively, of the load that you typically use for that exercise. Rest 1 to 3 minutes before starting your scheduled sets.

Lower-body exercises: 45 minutes

Number	Muscle group	Reps	Sets	Free weight	Pivot machine	Cam machine
1	Thighs	4-6	4*	Squat	Leg press	Horizontal leg press
2	Thighs	8-10	3	Angled leg press	Leg press	Horizontal leg press
3	Back of thigh	10-12	3	Leg (knee) curl	Leg (knee) curl	Leg (knee) curl
4	Front of thigh	10-12	3	Leg (knee) extension	Leg (knee) extension	Leg (knee) extension
5	Calf	10-12	3	Standing heel raise	Seated heel raise	Machine standing heel raise
6	Abdomen	15-25	3	Sit-up	Abdominal crunch	Abdominal crunch

Rest period: 3 minutes for exercise 1, 1 minute for all others

Cool-down: Slow walking for 5 minutes followed by stretching

Workout tips

* As you begin performing four sets in exercise 1, you may have to decrease the load by 10 pounds to complete all four sets.

Level 6 Workout 1

Total time: 1 hour, 38 minutes

Weeks: 1 and 2

Days of the week: Two nonconsecutive days

Warm-up: Easy jogging or rope skipping for 5 minutes followed by stretching. Before performing your first set of exercises 1 and 4, do three warm-up sets of 8 to 10, 6 to 8, and 4 to 6 repetitions with one-half, two-thirds, and three-quarters, respectively, of the load that you typically use for that exercise. Rest 1 to 4 minutes before starting your scheduled sets.

Upper-body exercises: 1 hour, 8 minutes

Number	Muscle group	Reps	Sets	Free weight	Pivot machine	Cam machine
1	Chest	2-4*	3	Bench press	Bench press	Chest press
2	Chest	10-12	3	Dumbbell fly	Pec deck	Pec deck
3	Back	10-12	3	Bent-over row	Lat pulldown	Seated row
4	Shoulders	2-4*	3	Standing press	Seated press	Shoulder press
5	Back	10-12	3	One-arm dumbbell row	Seated row	Lat pulldown
6	Back of arm	10-12	3	Lying triceps extension	Triceps pushdown	Triceps extension
7	Front of arm	10-12	3	Biceps curl	Low pulley curl	Preacher curl

Rest period: 4 minutes for exercises 1 and 4**; 1 minute for all others

Cool-down: Slow walking for 5 minutes followed by stretching

Workout tips

* In exercises 1 and 4 you will perform 2 to 4 reps. To do this, add 5 to 10 pounds to the loads from the level 5, workout 5 or consult chapter 5 for a more specific method for determining new loads.

** Notice that the heavier sets of 2 to 4 repetitions require more rest between sets and a spotter for the free-weight version of exercises 1 and 4.

Level 6　Workout 2

Total time: 1 hour, 17 minutes

Weeks: 1 and 2

Days of the week: Two nonconsecutive days

Warm-up: Easy jogging or rope skipping for 5 minutes followed by stretching. Before performing your first set of exercise 1, do three warm-up sets of 8 to 10, 6 to 8, and 4 to 6 repetitions with one-half, two-thirds, and three-quarters, respectively, of the load that you typically use for that exercise. Rest 1 to 4 minutes before starting your scheduled sets.

Lower-body exercises: 47 minutes

Number	Muscle group	Reps	Sets	Free weight	Pivot machine	Cam machine
1	Thighs	2-4*	3	Squat	Leg press	Horizontal leg press
2	Thighs	8-10	3	Angled leg press	Leg press	Horizontal leg press
3	Back of thigh	10-12	3	Leg (knee) curl	Leg (knee) curl	Leg (knee) curl
4	Front of thigh	10-12	3	Leg (knee) extension	Leg (knee) extension	Leg (knee) extension
5	Calf	10-12	3	Standing heel raise	Seated heel raise	Machine standing heel raise
6	Abdomen	15-25	3	Sit-up	Abdominal crunch	Abdominal crunch

Rest period: 4 minutes for exercise 1**; 1 minute for all others

Cool-down: Slow walking for 5 minutes followed by stretching

Workout tips

* In exercise 1 you will perform 2 to 4 reps. To do this, add 10 to 20 pounds to the load from the level 5, workout 6 or consult chapter 5 for a more specific method for determining new loads.

** Notice that the heavier sets of 2 to 4 repetitions require more rest between sets and a spotter for the free-weight version of exercises 1 and 2.

Level 6   Workout 3

Total time: 1 hour, 46 minutes

Weeks: 3 and 4

Days of the week: Two nonconsecutive days

Warm-up: Easy jogging or rope skipping for 5 minutes followed by stretching. Before performing your first set of exercises 1 and 4, do three warm-up sets of 8 to 10, 6 to 8, and 4 to 6 repetitions with one-half, two-thirds, and three-quarters, respectively, of the load that you typically use for that exercise. Rest 1 to 4 minutes before starting your scheduled sets.

Upper-body exercises: 1 hour, 16 minutes

Number	Muscle group	Reps	Sets	Free weight	Pivot machine	Cam machine
1	Chest	2-4	4*	Bench press	Bench press	Chest press
2	Chest	10-12	3	Dumbbell fly	Pec deck	Pec deck
3	Back	10-12	3	Bent-over row	Lat pulldown	Seated row
4	Shoulders	2-4	4*	Standing press	Seated press	Shoulder press
5	Back	10-12	3	One-arm dumbbell row	Seated row	Lat pulldown
6	Back of arm	10-12	3	Lying triceps extension	Triceps pushdown	Triceps extension
7	Front of arm	10-12	3	Biceps curl	Low pulley curl	Preacher curl

Rest period: 4 minutes for exercises 1 and 4; 1 minute for all others

Cool-down: Slow walking for 5 minutes followed by stretching

Workout tips

   * As you begin performing four sets in exercises 1 and 4, you may have to decrease the load by 5 pounds to complete all four sets.

Level 6   Workout 4

Total time: 1 hour, 21 minutes

Weeks: 3 and 4

Days of the week: Two nonconsecutive days

Warm-up: Easy jogging or rope skipping for 5 minutes followed by stretching. Before performing your first set of exercise 1, do three warm-up sets of 8 to 10, 6 to 8, and 4 to 6 repetitions with one-half, two-thirds, and three-quarters, respectively, of the load that you typically use for that exercise. Rest 1 to 4 minutes before starting your scheduled sets.

Lower-body exercises: 51 minutes

Number	Muscle group	Reps	Sets	Free weight	Pivot machine	Cam machine
1	Thighs	2-4	4*	Squat	Leg press	Horizontal leg press
2	Thighs	8-10	3	Angled leg press	Leg press	Horizontal leg press
3	Back of thigh	10-12	3	Leg (knee) curl	Leg (knee) curl	Leg (knee) curl
4	Front of thigh	10-12	3	Leg (knee) extension	Leg (knee) extension	Leg (knee) extension
5	Calf	10-12	3	Standing heel raise	Seated heel raise	Machine standing heel raise
6	Abdomen	15-25	3	Sit-up	Abdominal crunch	Abdominal crunch

Rest period: 4 minutes for exercise 1; 1 minute for all others

Cool-down: Slow walking for 5 minutes followed by stretching

Workout tips

* As you begin performing four sets in exercise 1, you may have to decrease the load by 10 pounds to complete all four sets.

Level 6   Workout 5

Total time: 1 hour, 55 minutes

Weeks: 5 and 6

Days of the week: Two nonconsecutive days

Warm-up: Easy jogging or rope skipping for 5 minutes followed by stretching. Before performing your first set of exercises 1 and 4, do three warm-up sets of 8 to 10, 6 to 8, and 4 to 6 repetitions with one-half, two-thirds, and three-quarters, respectively, of the load that you typically use for that exercise. Rest 1 to 4 minutes before starting your scheduled sets.

Upper-body exercises: 1 hour, 25 minutes

Number	Muscle group	Reps	Sets	Free weight	Pivot machine	Cam machine
1	Chest	2-4	5*	Bench press	Bench press	Chest press
2	Chest	10-12	3	Dumbbell fly	Pec deck	Pec deck
3	Back	10-12	3	Bent-over row	Lat pulldown	Seated row
4	Shoulders	2-4	5*	Standing press	Seated press	Shoulder press
5	Back	10-12	3	One-arm dumbbell row	Seated row	Lat pulldown
6	Back of arm	10-12	3	Lying triceps extension	Triceps pushdown	Triceps extension
7	Front of arm	10-12	3	Biceps curl	Low pulley curl	Preacher curl

Rest period: 4 minutes for exercises 1 and 4; 1 minute for all others

Cool-down: Slow walking for 5 minutes followed by stretching

Workout tips

* As you begin performing five sets in exercises 1 and 4, you may have to decrease the load by 5 pounds to complete all five sets.

Level 6   Workout 6

Total time: 1 hour, 26 minutes

Weeks: 5 and 6

Days of the week: Two nonconsecutive days

Warm-up: Easy jogging or rope skipping for 5 minutes followed by stretching. Before performing your first set of exercise 1, do three warm-up sets of 8 to 10, 6 to 8, and 4 to 6 repetitions with one-half, two-thirds, and three-quarters, respectively, of the load that you typically use for that exercise. Rest 1 to 4 minutes before starting your scheduled sets.

Lower-body exercises: 56 minutes

Number	Muscle group	Reps	Sets	Free weight	Pivot machine	Cam machine
1	Thighs	2-4	5*	Squat	Leg press	Horizontal leg press
2	Thighs	8-10	3	Angled leg press	Leg press	Horizontal leg press
3	Back of thigh	10-12	3	Leg (knee) curl	Leg (knee) curl	Leg (knee) curl
4	Front of thigh	10-12	3	Leg (knee) extension	Leg (knee) extension	Leg (knee) extension
5	Calf	10-12	3	Standing heel raise	Seated heel raise	Machine standing heel raise
6	Abdomen	15-25	3	Sit-up	Abdominal crunch	Abdominal crunch

Rest period: 4 minutes for exercise 1; 1 minute for all others

Cool-down: Slow walking for 5 minutes followed by stretching

Workout tips

* As you begin performing five sets in exercise 1, you may have to decrease the load by 10 pounds to complete all five sets.

Weight Training Exercises

The following pages illustrate the most commonly accepted movement techniques for the exercises contained in the workouts in chapters 7, 8, and 9. The exercises are arranged according to body areas and exercise type: free-weight (FW), pivot machine (PM), cam machine (CM), and resistance band (RB) exercises. The first figure is the initial, or start, position, and the second figure shows the action by way of movement arrows (if needed). In exercises for which a spotter is recommended, the spotter's role in the action is illustrated.

Weight Training Exercises

Abdomen

Sit-up (FW) 141

Abdominal crunch
(PM, CM) 142

Back of the Arms (Triceps)

Dumbbell triceps extension
(FW) 143

Lying triceps extension
(FW) 144

Triceps pushdown (PM) 145

Triceps extension (CM) 146

One-arm triceps extension
(RB) 147

Front of the Arms (Biceps)

Biceps curl (FW) 148

Dumbbell biceps curl (FW) 149

Low pulley curl (PM) 150

Preacher curl (CM) 151

Biceps curl (RB) 152

Back

Bent-over row (FW) 153

One-arm dumbbell row
(FW) 154

Seated row (PM, CM) 155

Lat pulldown (PM, CM) 156

Machine pullover (CM) 157

Seated row (RB) 158

Calves

Standing heel raise (FW) 159

Standing heel raise (PM) 160

Seated heel raise (PM) 161

Chest

Bench press (FW) 162

Dumbbell fly (FW) 163

Bench press (PM) 164

Chest press (CM) 166

Pec deck (PM, CM) 167

Chest press (RB) 168

Thigh

Squat (FW) 169

Lunge (FW) 171

Angled leg press (FW) 172

Leg press (PM) 174

Horizontal leg press
(PM, CM) 174

Squat (RB) 176

Back of the Thigh (Hamstrings)

Leg (knee) curl (PM, CM) 177

Front of the Thigh (Quadriceps)

Leg (knee) extension
(PM, CM) 179

Shoulders

Standing press (FW) 180

Dumbbell lateral raise
(FW) 182

Seated (or shoulder) press
(PM, CM) 183

Shoulder press (RB) 184

Lateral raise (RB) 185

Whole Body

Power clean (FW) 186

Abdomen

Sit-Up (FW)

Major muscle trained: rectus abdominis

Initial position
- Lie face up on a floor mat.
- Flex the knees and cross the arms across the chest or abdomen.

Upward movement
- Curl the torso toward the thighs until the upper back is off the mat.
- Keep the feet flat on the mat.

Downward movement
- Allow the torso to uncurl back to the initial position.
- Do not let the hips lift off the mat.

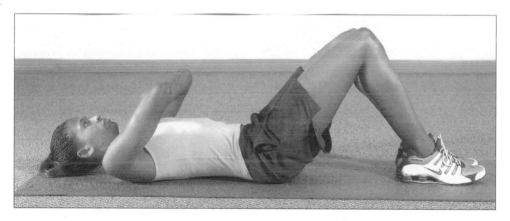

Abdominal Crunch (PM, CM)

Major muscle trained: rectus abdominis

Initial position

- Sit in the machine with the upper chest pressed against the pad or hold the handles with a closed, pronated grip.

Forward movement

- Lean forward to curl or flex the torso toward the thighs.

Backward movement

- Allow the torso to move backward back to the initial position.

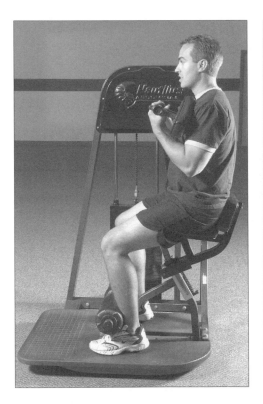
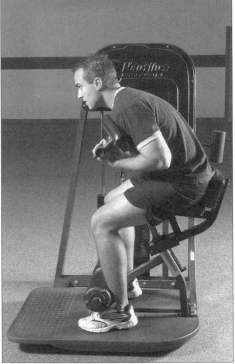

Back of the Arms (Triceps)

Dumbbell Triceps Extension (FW)

Major muscle trained: triceps brachii

Initial position

- Stand on the right side of a flat bench and kneel on the bench with the left leg.
- Flex forward and position the left hand on the bench in front of the left knee so that the arm and thigh are parallel to each other.
- Slightly flex the right knee and keep this position during the whole exercise.
- Reach down and pick up a dumbbell using a closed, neutral grip.
- Lift the dumbbell up and flex the right elbow 90 degrees to position the upper arm next to the torso with the dumbbell hanging straight down from the elbow.

Upward movement

- Extend the right elbow until the arm is straight and parallel to the floor.
- Keep the upper part of the right arm against the torso as you extend the elbow.
- Be sure to keep the wrists straight.
- Do not allow the rest of the body to move.

Downward movement

- Allow the elbow to flex to lower the dumbbell back to the initial position.
- Do not allow the rest of the body to move.
- When you complete the set, stand on the left side of the bench and repeat the movement with the left arm.

143

Lying Triceps Extension (FW)

Major muscle trained: triceps brachii

Note: This exercise requires a spotter.

Initial position

- Lie face up on a bench with the head, back, and buttocks in contact with the bench and the feet flat on the floor.
- Take the bar from the spotter with a closed, pronated grip about shoulder-width (or slightly narrower) apart.
- Hold the bar over the chest with the elbows extended.

Downward movement

- Allow the elbows to flex to lower the bar almost to touch the top of the head.

- Keep the arms parallel to each other; don't let the elbows flare out as you flex them.
- Keep the head, back, and buttocks in contact with the bench and the feet flat on the floor.

Upward movement

- Extend the elbows back to the initial position.
- Keep the arms parallel to each other and perpendicular to the bench.
- Keep the head, back, and buttocks in contact with the bench and the feet flat on the floor.
- When you complete the set, allow the spotter to take the bar from your hands.

Triceps Pushdown (PM)

Major muscle trained: triceps brachii

Initial position

- Face the machine and stand almost directly under the hanging bar.
- Grasp the bar with a closed, pronated grip slightly narrower than shoulder-width.
- Place the feet shoulder-width apart with the knees slightly flexed.
- Pull the bar down and place the upper arms against the sides of the torso.
- Stand erect with the cable in front of your nose.

Downward movement

- Extend the elbows until they are fully extended.
- Do not allow the rest of the body to move.

Upward movement

- Allow the elbows to flex back to the initial position.
- When you are finished, raise the arms up to set the weight back down to its resting position.

Triceps Extension (CM)

Major muscle trained: triceps brachii

Initial position

- Sit in the machine, press the chest against the pad, and place the feet flat on the floor.
- Grasp the handles using a closed, pronated (or neutral) grip with the elbows fully flexed.
- Move the upper arms on the arm pad or pads to be parallel with each other with the elbows lined up with the axis of the machine.

Downward movement

- Push the handles away from the shoulders until the elbows are fully extended.
- Keep the chest and upper arms pressed against the pads.

Upward movement

- Allow the elbows to flex back to the initial position.

One-Arm Triceps Extension (RB)

Major muscle trained: triceps brachii

Initial position

- Grasp the handles of the band with a closed, pronated grip.
- Sit erect on the floor with the legs out in front of you with the knees flexed and feet on the floor.
- Position the body and the band so that you are sitting on top of the middle of the band.
- Flex the elbows to move the arms and band handles behind the head and upper back with the palms facing forward.

Upward movement

- Extend the right elbow until the hand is over the head.
- Do not let the wrist move and keep the upper arm next to the head.

Downward movement

- Allow the elbow to flex to move the handle down to the initial position.
- Repeat the exercise with the left arm and continue by alternating arms.

Front of the Arms (Biceps)

Biceps Curl (FW)

Major muscle trained: biceps brachii

Initial position

- Pick up the bar using a closed, supinated grip shoulder-width apart.
- Slightly flex the knees and position the bar in front of the thighs with the elbows extended.

Upward movement

- Flex the elbows to raise the bar toward the shoulders.
- Keep the upper arms pressed against the torso.

Downward movement

- Allow the elbows to extend back to the initial position.
- Be sure to lower the bar until the elbows are fully extended.

Dumbbell Biceps Curl (FW)

Major muscle trained: biceps brachii

Initial position

- Pick up two dumbbells using a closed, neutral grip.
- Slightly flex the knees and position the dumbbells on the sides of the thighs with the elbows extended.

Upward movement

- Flex the right elbow to raise the dumbbell upward, turning the palm up as the dumbbell moves closer to the right shoulder.
- Keep the upper arm pressed against the torso.

Downward movement

- Allow the elbow to extend back to the initial position.
- Be sure to lower the dumbbell until the right elbow is fully extended
- Repeat the exercise with the left arm and continue by alternating arms.

Low Pulley Curl (PM)

Major muscle trained: biceps brachii

Initial position

- Stand in front (or sit in the attached seat) of a low pulley station.
- Pick up the bar using a closed, supinated grip shoulder-width apart.
- Slightly flex the knees and position the bar in front of the thighs with the elbows extended.

Upward movement

- Flex the elbows to raise the bar toward the shoulders.
- Keep the upper arms pressed against the torso.

Downward movement

- Allow the elbows to extend back to the initial position.
- Be sure to lower the bar until the elbows are fully extended.

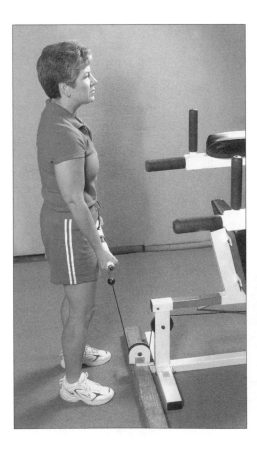

Preacher Curl (CM)

Major muscle trained: biceps brachii

Initial position

- Sit in the machine, press the chest against the pad, and place the feet flat on the floor.
- Grasp the handles using a closed, supinated grip with the elbows fully extended.
- Move the upper arms on the arm pad or pads to be parallel with each other with the elbows lined up with the axis of the machine.

Upward movement

- Flex the elbows to raise the handles toward the shoulders.
- Keep the chest and upper arms pressed against the pads.

Downward movement

- Allow the elbows to extend back to the initial position.
- Be sure to lower the handles until the elbows are fully extended.

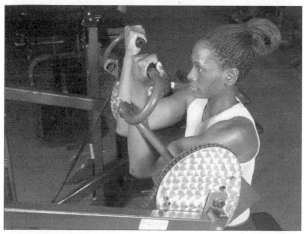

Biceps Curl (RB)

Major muscle trained: biceps brachii

Initial position

- Grasp the handles of the band with a closed, supinated grip.
- Stand on top of the middle of the band with the feet shoulder-width apart.
- Move the arms and band handles on the outside of the thighs with the palms facing forward.

Upward movement

- Flex the elbows to raise the band handles toward the shoulders.
- Keep the body erect with the knees slightly flexed and feet flat on the floor.

Downward movement

- Allow the elbows to extend to move the handles down to the initial position.

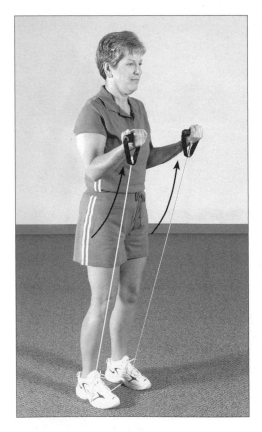

- Be sure to lower the band handles until the elbows are fully extended.
- Keep the body erect with the knees slightly flexed and feet flat on the floor.

Back

Bent-Over Row (FW)

Major muscles trained: latissimus dorsi, rhomboids

Initial position

- Pick up the bar (with the legs, as in the squat exercise) using a closed, pronated grip wider than shoulder-width apart.
- Slightly flex the knees and position the bar in front of the thighs with the elbows extended.
- Flex the knees about one-quarter of the way and keep this position during the whole exercise.
- Flex forward to position the upper body slightly above parallel to the floor.
- Be sure you keep the upper back flat, not rounded or hunched over.
- Let the bar hang straight down with the elbows fully extended.

Upward movement

- Pull up on the bar to lift it to touch the lower chest or the upper part of the abdomen.
- Be sure to keep the wrists straight, not curling the bar in the hands.
- Do not allow the rest of the body to move.

Downward movement

- Allow the elbows to extend to lower the bar back to the initial position.
- Do not allow the rest of the body to move.
- When you complete the set, place the bar down on the floor using a squatting movement.

One-Arm Dumbbell Row (FW)

Major muscles trained: latissimus dorsi, rhomboids

Initial position

- Stand on the right side of a flat bench and kneel on the bench with the left leg.
- Flex forward and position the left hand on the bench in front of the left knee so that the arm and thigh are parallel to each other.
- Slightly flex the right knee and keep this position during the whole exercise.
- Reach down and pick up a dumbbell using a closed, neutral grip.

- Let the right arm and dumbbell hang straight down.

Upward movement

- Pull up on the dumbbell to lift it to touch the right side of the torso.
- Brush the upper part of the right arm against the torso as you pull up on the dumbbell.
- Be sure to keep the wrists straight, not curling the dumbbell in the hands.
- Do not allow the rest of the body to move.

Downward movement

- Allow the elbow to extend to lower the dumbbell back to the initial position.
- Do not allow the rest of the body to move.
- When you complete the set, stand on the left side of the bench and repeat the movement with the left arm.

Seated Row (PM, CM)

Major muscles trained: latissimus dorsi, rhomboids

Initial position

- Sit in the machine, press the chest against the pad, and place the feet flat on the floor. If you are sitting on a long pad or on the floor (see photos), there will not be a chest pad.
- Place the feet flat on the floor (if you are in a machine) or on the foot supports (if there is no chest pad).
- If you are sitting on a long pad or on the floor, flex the knees slightly and keep this position during the whole exercise.
- Grasp the handles or short bar using a closed, pronated (or neutral) grip with the elbows fully extended.
- Position the upper body perpendicular to the floor.
- Be sure you keep the upper back flat, not rounded or hunched over.

Backward movement

- Pull the handles or short bar toward the lower chest or the upper part of the abdomen.
- Be sure to keep the wrists straight, not curling the bar in the hands.
- Do not allow the rest of the body to move.

Forward movement

- Allow the elbows to extend back to the initial position.
- Do not allow the rest of the body to move.

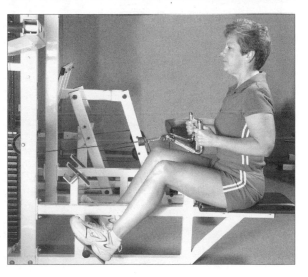

Lat Pulldown (PM, CM)

Major muscles trained: latissimus dorsi, rhomboids

Initial position

- Kneel in front (or sit in the attached seat) of a high pulley station.
- Reach up and grasp up the long bar using a closed, pronated grip wider than shoulder-width apart.
- With the elbows fully extended, lean the upper body back slightly so that you can see the bar above your face.

Downward movement

- Pull the bar down so that it passes close to the chin and touches the upper part of the chest.
- Do not allow the rest of the body to move.

Upward movement

- Allow the elbows to extend to let the bar move up back to the initial position.
- Do not allow the rest of the body to move.

Machine Pullover (CM)

Major muscle trained: latissimus dorsi

Initial position

- Sit in the machine; press the upper back and hips against the pads; and place the feet flat on the floor, if possible.
- Position the body with the shoulders lined up with the axis of the machine.
- Grasp the handles using a closed, pronated (or neutral) grip with the upper arms on the arm pads.

Downward movement

- Pull the bar down in a wide arc by pressing down on the arm pads and pulling with the hands.
- Keep the feet on the floor and the upper back and hips pressed against the pads.

Upward movement

- Allow the arms to move back to the initial position.
- Keep the feet on the floor and the upper back and hips pressed against the pads.

Seated Row (RB)

Major muscles trained: latissimus dorsi, rhomboids

Initial position

- Grasp the handles of the band with a closed, pronated (or neutral) grip.
- Sit on the floor with the legs out in front of you with the knees straight.
- Evenly wrap the band around the instep of the feet so that the band is taut and the elbows are fully extended.
- Be sure you keep the upper back flat, not rounded or hunched over.

Backward movement

- Pull the handles toward the sides of the torso and ribs.
- Be sure to keep the wrists straight, not curling the handle in the hands.
- Do not allow the rest of the body to move.

Forward movement

- Allow the elbows to extend back to the initial position.
- Do not allow the rest of the body to move.

Calves

Standing Heel Raise (FW)

Major muscles trained: soleus, gastrocnemius

Initial position

- Use a bar held in the hands and placed across the back of the shoulders (as in the squat exercise) or one or two dumbbells held at arm's length at the side or sides.
- Place the balls of the feet on the closest edge of a step, platform, or board with the feet parallel to each other.
- Allow the heels to drop down lower than the step, platform, or board until you feel a slight stretch.
- Be sure not to allow the knees to lock out forcefully, but they should be straight.

Upward movement

- Point the toes to lift the heels off the floor.
- Keep the body fully erect; be sure not to look down or lean forward or backward.

Downward movement

- Allow the heels to drop back down to the initial position.
- Keep the body fully erect; be sure not to look down or lean forward or backward.

Standing Heel Raise (PM)

Major muscles trained: soleus, gastrocnemius

Initial position

- Face the machine and place the balls of the feet on the closest edge of a step, platform, or board with the feet parallel to each other.
- Dip the body under the shoulder pads and stand up with the body fully erect.
- Allow the heels to drop down lower than the step until you feel a slight stretch.
- Be sure not to allow the knees to lock out.

Upward movement

- Point the toes to lift the heels off the floor.
- Keep the body fully erect; be sure not to look down or lean forward or backward.

Downward movement

- Allow the heels to drop back down to the initial position.
- Keep the body fully erect; be sure not to look down or lean forward or backward.

 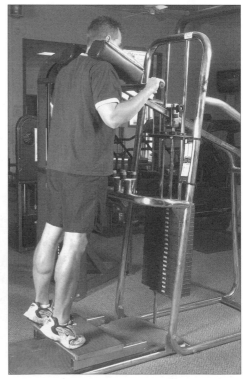

Seated Heel Raise (PM)

Major muscles trained: soleus, gastrocnemius

Initial position

- Sit in the machine and place the knees and thighs under the pads.
- Position the balls of the feet on the closest edge of the step with the feet parallel to each other.
- Slightly point the toes to lift the thigh pads so that you can move the support bar out of the way.
- Allow the heels to drop down lower than the step until you feel a slight stretch.

Upward movement

- Point the toes to lift the heels up.
- Be sure not to pull on the handles or lean the torso backward.

Downward movement

- Allow the heels to drop back down to the initial position.
- When you complete the set, move the support bar back into place.

Chest

Bench Press (FW)

Major muscle trained: pectoralis major

Note: This exercise requires a spotter.

Initial position

- Lie face up on a bench with the head, back, and buttocks in contact with the bench and the feet flat on the floor. The bar should be over the eyes when you look at the ceiling.

- Grasp the bar with a closed, pronated grip slightly wider than shoulder width.
- With the spotter's assistance, lift the bar off the racks and move it into a position over the chest with the elbows fully extended.

Downward movement

- Allow the elbows to flex to lower the bar to touch the middle of the chest.
- Keep a firm grip on the bar with the forearms approximately perpendicular to the floor and parallel to each other.
- Keep the head, back, and buttocks in contact with the bench and the feet flat on the floor.

Upward movement

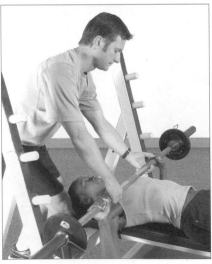

- Push the bar up until the elbows are fully extended (the initial position).
- Keep the head, back, and buttocks in contact with the bench and the feet flat on the floor.
- When you complete the set, move the bar back on the racks with the spotter's assistance.

Dumbbell Fly (FW)

Major muscle trained: pectoralis major

Note: This exercise requires a spotter (not shown, for ease in viewing technique).

Initial position

- Lie face up on a bench with the head, back, and buttocks in contact with the bench and the feet flat on the floor.
- Take the dumbbells (or have them already in your hands) from the spotter with a closed grip.
- Move the dumbbells to the chest and press them straight up until the arms are fully extended.
- Rotate the dumbbells so that the palms face each other and the elbows point out to the sides.
- As you begin the exercise, slightly flex the elbows and keep them in this slightly flexed position during the whole exercise.

Downward movement

- Allow the dumbbells to lower at the same rate in a wide arc until they are level with the torso.
- Keep the palms facing each other and the elbows slightly flexed.
- Keep the dumbbells and the elbows and shoulders in one vertical plane.
- Keep the head, back, and buttocks in contact with the bench and the feet flat on the floor.

Upward movement

- Raise the dumbbells up and toward each other in a wide arc back to the initial position.
- Keep the palms facing each other and the elbows slightly flexed.
- Keep the dumbbells and the elbows and shoulders in one vertical plane.
- Keep the head, back, and buttocks in contact with the bench and the feet flat on the floor.
- When you complete the set, allow the spotter to take the dumbbells from the hands or set them on the floor yourself.

Bench Press (PM)

Major muscle trained: pectoralis major

Initial position

- Lie face up on a bench with the head, back, and buttocks in contact with the bench and the feet flat on the floor. The handles should line up with the middle of the chest.
- Grasp the handles with a closed, pronated grip slightly wider than shoulder width.

Upward movement

- Push the handles up until the elbows are fully extended.
- Keep the forearms approximately perpendicular to the floor and parallel to each other.
- Keep the head, back, and buttocks in contact with the bench and the feet flat on the floor.

Downward movement

- Allow the elbows to flex to lower the handles to the initial position.
- Keep a firm grip on the handles with the forearms approximately perpendicular to the floor and parallel to each other.
- Keep the head, back, and buttocks in contact with the bench and the feet flat on the floor.

Chest Press (CM)

Major muscle trained: pectoralis major

Initial position
- Sit in the machine; press the head, upper back, and hips against the pads; and place the feet flat on the floor. The handles should line up with the middle of the chest.
- Grasp the handles with a closed, pronated (or neutral) grip slightly wider than shoulder width.

Forward movement
- Push the handles away from the body until the elbows are fully extended.
- Keep the head, back, and buttocks in contact with the pads and the feet flat on the floor.

Backward movement
- Allow the elbows to flex to move the handles back to the initial position.
- Keep the head, back, and buttocks in contact with the pads and the feet flat on the floor.

Pec Deck (PM, CM)

Major muscle trained: pectoralis major

Initial position

- Sit in the machine; press the head, upper back, and hips against the pads; and place the feet flat on the floor.
- Grasp the handles or pads and press the forearms against the arm pads (if any); in this position, the elbows will be flexed about 90 degrees and the upper arms should be no higher than parallel with the floor.

Forward movement

- Move the handles or pads toward each other in a wide arc by squeezing the forearms and elbows together.
- Continue to move the handles or pads together until they touch in front of the face.
- Keep the feet on the floor and the head pressed against the pad

Backward movement

- Allow the arms to move out and back to the initial position.
- Keep the feet on the floor and the upper back and hips pressed against the pads.

Chest Press (RB)

Major muscle trained: pectoralis major

Initial position

- Grasp the handles of the band with a closed, pronated (or neutral) grip.
- Evenly wrap the band around the torso at midchest level.
- Stand erect with the feet shoulder-width apart and the knees slightly flexed.
- Move the handles to the sides of the torso at midchest height with the palms facing the floor.

Forward movement

- Push the handles away from the chest until the elbows are fully extended.
- Keep the arms parallel to the floor and do not allow the rest of the body to move.

Backward movement

- Allow the elbows to flex back to the initial position.
- Keep the arms parallel to the floor and do not allow the rest of the body to move.

Thigh

Squat (FW)

Major muscles trained: gluteus maximus, hamstrings, quadriceps

Note: This exercise requires at least one spotter.

Initial position

- If the bar begins in a rack, step under the middle of it and position the feet parallel to each other directly under the bar. If you have to lift the bar off the floor first, follow the guidelines for the power clean exercise first, then use a spotter to help place bar over head and on to back of shoulders.

- Grasp the bar with a closed, pronated grip slightly wider than shoulder width.

- Position the body so that you can place the bar evenly on the upper back at the base of the neck and across the back of the shoulders.

- Slightly arch the back so that it is flat and tilt the head slightly backward.

- With the spotter's assistance, extend the hips and knees to lift the bar off the racks and take one or two steps backward.

- Reposition the feet to be approximately shoulder-width apart with the toes pointed slightly outward.

- Re-arch the back so that it is still flat, not rounded.

Downward movement

- Allow the hips and knees to flex at the same rate to keep the near-erect flat-back position.
- Be sure to keep the heels in full contact with the floor and the knees aligned over the feet.
- Continue the downward movement until the thighs are parallel to the floor (but if the heels lift off the floor or you begin to lean forward, you are too low).

Upward movement

- Extend the hips and knees (at the same rate) to stand back up to the initial position.
- Be sure to keep the back flat, the heels on the floor, and the knees aligned over the feet.
- When you complete the set, step forward and allow the spotter to help you rack the bar.

Lunge (FW)

Major muscles trained: gluteus maximus, hamstrings, quadriceps

Note: This exercise requires a spotter (not shown, for ease of viewing technique).

Initial position

- Grasp the bar with a closed, pronated grip slightly wider than shoulder width. (The other option is to use dumbbells held in a neutral grip on the outside of both thighs.)
- Position the body so that you can place the bar evenly on the upper back at the base of the neck and across the back of the shoulders.
- Slightly arch the back so that it is flat and tilt the head slightly backward.
- Position the feet to be approximately shoulder-width apart with the toes slightly pointed outward.

Forward movement

- Take one exaggerated step directly ahead with the right leg.
- Keep the left leg and foot in the initial position but allow the left knee to flex as you step forward.
- Place the right foot squarely on the floor with the toes pointing straight ahead or slightly inward.
- When both feet are in firm contact with the floor (the whole right foot and the ball of the left foot), flex the right knee to lower the left knee toward the floor.
- Allow the right hip and knee to flex as you lunge forward and down.

- Continue lunging until the left knee is close to the floor but not touching it.
- Be sure that the right knee does not flex past the toes of the right foot.
- Be sure to keep the torso erect and the bar firmly on the shoulders.

Backward movement

- Push off the floor by extending the right hip and knee. The left hip and knee will extend also.
- Continue to lunge back until both feet are back to the initial position.
- Be sure to keep the torso erect and the bar firmly on the shoulders.
- Repeat the exercise with the left leg taking the exaggerated step and continue by alternating legs.

Angled Leg Press (FW)

Major muscles trained: gluteus maximus, hamstrings, quadriceps

Initial position

- Sit in the machine with the head, back, and buttocks in contact with the pads.
- Position the feet hip-width apart and in the middle of the foot platform.
- Position the thighs and lower legs parallel to each other.
- Slightly extend the hips and knees to lift the foot platform so that you can move the support bar out of the way.
- Grasp the handles or the side of the seat and fully extend the hips and knees.

Downward movement

- Allow the hips and knees to flex at the same rate to keep the back and buttocks in contact with the pads.
- Be sure to keep the heels in full contact with the foot platform and the knees aligned with the feet.
- Continue the downward movement until the thighs are parallel to the foot platform (but if the heels lift off the platform or the hips or buttocks lose contact with the seat, you are too low).

Upward movement

- Extend the hips and knees to push the foot platform back up to the initial position.
- Be sure to keep the heels in full contact with the foot platform and the knees aligned with the feet.
- When you complete the set, move the support bar back into place.

Leg Press (PM)

Major muscles trained: gluteus maximus, hamstrings, quadriceps

Initial position

- Sit in the machine with the back and buttocks in contact with the seat pads.
- Place the feet on the foot pedals. If possible, change the seat position so that in the initial position the thighs are parallel to the foot pedals.
- Position the thighs and lower legs parallel to each other.
- Grasp the handles or the side of the seat.

Forward movement

- Extend the hips and knees to push the foot pedals away from you.
- Be sure to keep the heels in full contact with the foot pedals, the knees aligned with the feet, and the back and buttocks in contact with the seat pads.
- Continue to push the foot pedals forward until the knees are fully extended.

Backward movement

- Allow the hips and knees to flex to return the foot pedals to the initial position.
- Keep the hips and buttocks on the seat and the back flat against the back pad.

Horizontal Leg Press (PM, CM)

Major muscles trained: gluteus maximus, hamstrings, quadriceps

Initial position

- Lie in the machine with the head, back, and buttocks in contact with the pads.
- Position the feet hip-width apart and in the middle of the foot platform. If possible, change the seat position or the foot platform so that in the initial position the thighs are parallel to the foot platform.
- Position the thighs and lower legs parallel to each other.
- Grasp the handles or the sides of the seat.

Forward movement

- Extend the hips and knees to push the foot pedals away from you (some machines may have a fixed foot platform with a seat that moves backward).
- Be sure to keep the heels in full contact with the foot pedals; the knees aligned with the feet; and the head, back, and buttocks in contact with the pads.
- Continue to push the foot platform forward until the knees are fully extended.

Backward movement

- Allow the hips and knees to flex to return the foot pedals to the initial position.
- Keep the head, back, and buttocks in contact with the pads.

Squat (RB)

Major muscles trained: gluteus maximus, hamstrings, quadriceps

Initial position
- Grasp the handles of the band with a closed, pronated grip.
- Stand on top of the middle of the band with the feet shoulder-width apart.
- Slightly arch the back so that it is flat and tilt the head slightly backward.
- Flex the hips and knees to squat down so that the thighs are parallel to the floor.
- Move the arms to position the handles to the outside of the shoulders with the palms facing upward.

Upward movement
- Extend the hips and knees at the same rate to keep the near-erect flat-back position.
- Keep the heels in full contact with the floor and the knees aligned over the feet.
- Continue the upward movement until you are standing.

Downward movement
- Allow the hips and knees to flex at the same rate back to the initial position.
- Keep the heels in full contact with the floor and the knees aligned over the feet.

Back of the Thigh (Hamstrings)

Leg (Knee) Curl (PM, CM)

Major muscle trained: hamstrings

Initial position

- Lie face down in the machine with the torso and thighs positioned on the pads so that the knees are aligned with the axis of the machine.
- Position the heels under the ankle pad or pads with the lower part of the calf or back of the heels pressing against the pad or pads.
- Be sure that the thighs, lower legs, and feet are parallel to each other.
- Grasp the handles or the sides of the torso pad.

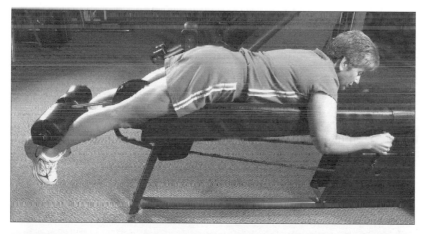

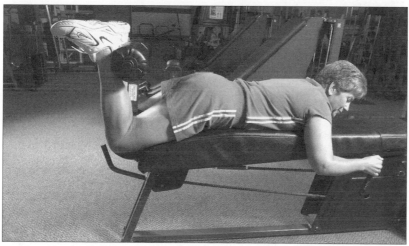

Upward movement

- Flex the knees until the ankle pad or pads nearly touch the buttocks.
- Keep the thighs, lower legs, and feet parallel to each other.
- Do not allow the rest of the body to move.

Downward movement

- Allow the knees to extend back to the initial position.
- Keep the thighs, lower legs, and feet parallel to each other.
- Do not allow the rest of the body to move.

Front of the Thigh (Quadriceps)

Leg (Knee) Extension (PM, CM)

Major muscle trained: quadriceps

Initial position

- Sit in the machine with the back and thighs positioned in the seat so that the knees are aligned with the axis of the machine.
- Position the feet under the ankle pad or pads with the instep of the feet pressing against the pad or pads.
- Be sure that the thighs, lower legs, and feet are parallel to each other.
- Grasp the handles or the sides of the seat.

Upward movement

- Extend the knees until they are straight.
- Keep the thighs, lower legs, and feet parallel to each other.
- Do not allow the rest of the body to move.

Downward movement

- Allow the knees to flex back to the initial position.
- Keep the thighs, lower legs, and feet parallel to each other.
- Do not allow the rest of the body to move.

Shoulders

Standing Press (FW)

Major muscle trained: deltoids

Note: This exercise requires a spotter.

Initial position

- If the bar begins in a rack, step under the middle of it and position the feet parallel to each other directly under the bar. If you have to lift the bar off the floor first, follow the guidelines for the power clean exercise first.
- Grasp and position it at the clavicles and the front of the shoulders with a closed, pronated grip slightly wider than shoulder width.
- Slightly arch the back so that it is flat and the torso is erect.
- Position the feet to be approximately shoulder-width apart.
- As you begin the exercise, tilt the head slightly backward.

Upward movement

- Push the bar straight up (just missing the chin) until the elbows are fully extended.
- Keep the wrists straight and directly above the elbows.
- Do not tilt the head too far back or lean backward as you press the bar overhead.

Downward movement

- Allow the elbows to flex to lower the bar back to the initial position. Be sure to tilt the head slightly so that the bar does not hit the head, nose, or chin.
- Keep the wrists straight and directly above the elbows.

Dumbbell Lateral Raise (FW)

Major muscle trained: deltoids

Initial position
- Pick up two dumbbells using a closed, neutral grip.
- Slightly flex the knees and position the dumbbells on the front of the thighs with the palms facing each other.
- Slightly flex the elbows and keep them in this slightly flexed position during the whole exercise.

Upward movement
- Lift the dumbbells up and out to the sides with the hands, forearms, elbows, and upper arms rising together.
- Keep the body erect with the knees slightly flexed and feet flat on the floor.
- Continue lifting the dumbbells until the arms are parallel to the floor or nearly level with the shoulders.

Downward movement
- Lower the dumbbells to the initial position.
- Keep the body erect with the knees slightly flexed and feet flat on the floor.

Seated (or Shoulder) Press (PM, CM)

Major muscle trained: deltoids

Initial position

- Sit in the machine; press the head, upper back, and hips against the pads; and place the feet flat on the floor. The handles should line up with the top of the shoulders.

- Grasp the handles with a closed, pronated (or neutral) grip slightly wider than shoulder width.

Upward movement

- Push the handles upward until the elbows are fully extended.

- Keep the head, back, and buttocks in contact with the pads and the feet flat on the floor.

Downward movement

- Allow the elbows to flex to move the handles back to the initial position.

- Keep the head, back, and buttocks in contact with the pads and the feet flat on the floor

Shoulder Press (RB)

Major muscle trained: deltoids

Initial position

- Grasp the handles of the band with a closed, pronated grip.
- Sit erect on the floor with the legs out in front of you.
- Position the body and the band so that you are sitting on top of the middle of the band.
- Position the band handles to line up with the top of the shoulders with the palms facing forward.

Upward movement

- Push the handles upward until the elbows are fully extended.
- Keep the body erect with the wrists straight and directly above the elbows.

Downward movement

- Allow the handles to move back down to the initial position.
- Keep the body erect with the wrists straight and directly above the elbows.

Lateral Raise (RB)

Major muscle trained: deltoids

Initial position

- Grasp the handles of the band with a closed, neutral grip.
- Stand on top of the middle of the band with the feet shoulder-width apart.
- Move the arms and band handles to the outside of the thighs with the palms facing inward.

Upward movement

- Lift the handles up and out to the sides with the hands, forearms, elbows, and upper arms rising together.
- Keep the body erect with the knees slightly flexed and feet flat on the floor.
- Continue lifting the handles until the arms are parallel to the floor or nearly level with the shoulders

Downward movement

- Allow the handles to lower to the initial position.
- Keep the body erect with the knees slightly flexed and feet flat on the floor.

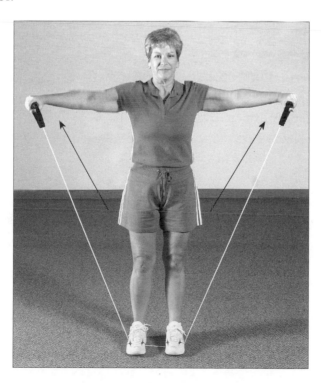

Whole Body

Power Clean (FW)

Major muscles trained: gluteus maximus, hamstrings, quadriceps, soleus, gastrocnemius, deltoids, trapezius

Initial position

- Stand with the feet hip-width apart with the toes pointed slightly outward.
- Squat down with the hips lower than the shoulders and grasp the bar with a closed, pronated grip about shoulder-width apart, outside the knees, with the elbows fully extended.
- Place the feet flat on the floor and position the bar over the balls of the feet.
- Slightly arch the back so that it is flat and tilt the head slightly backward. See photo *a*.

Upward movement: first pull

- Rapidly extend the hips and knees at the same rate to keep the near-erect flat-back position and the bar close to the shins.
- Be sure to keep the heels in full contact with the floor and the knees aligned over the feet.
- Keep the elbows fully extended and the shoulders over or slightly ahead of the bar. See photo *b*.

Upward movement: scoop (transition)

- As the bar rises just above the knees, move the hips forward and quickly flex the knees to move them under the bar.
- Keep the near-erect flat-back position with the elbows still fully extended. See photo *c*.

Upward movement: second pull

- Immediately after the knees move under the bar, rapidly jump up by extending the hips and knees pointing the feet and ankles.
- Keep the bar near the body and maintain the near-erect flat-back position with the elbows still extended.
- After you fully extend the hips, knees, and ankles, rapidly shrug the shoulders with the elbows still extended.
- After you fully shrug the shoulders, flex the elbows to continue moving the bar upward. See photo *d*.

Upward movement: catch

- After the bar reaches its maximum height, rotate the arms around and then under the bar and, at the same time, flex the hips and knees into a quarter-squat position.
- Catch the bar at the clavicles and the front of the shoulders with the upper arms parallel to the floor. Be sure that the torso is in a near-erect flat-back position when you catch the bar. See photo *e*.
- After you catch the bar, stand up by extending the hips and knees.

Downward movement

- Reverse the arm and leg movements to allow the bar to move back down first to the thighs and then to the initial position on the floor.

a

b

c   *d*   *e*

Designing Weight Training Programs

If you are reading this section, you have probably completed the level 6 workout and are ready for more! You may want to design your own program, calculating proper loads and choosing exercises. Instructions for program design are discussed in chapter 11, along with information on how to make program adjustments for continued improvement. Or, like many people, you are interested in participating in a variety of activities along with weight training. If so, chapter 12 describes how to design a workout plan that mixes in aerobic exercise (like walking, running, biking, or swimming) with your weight training program. If you already participate in a certain sport or activity, go to chapter 13 to learn how to modify your current weight training program (or one found in chapters 7 through 9 or even chapter 12) to enhance your performance.

Apply the Specificity Principle

By now, you understand the purpose of following a well-designed weight training program; besides minimizing injury or overuse, adhering to an effective program will help you meet your desired training goal more quickly than you will by doing "any ol' thing" in the weight room. Recall that chapter 4 contained several questions to help you focus on your primary training goal. A well-designed weight training program is based on the principle of *specificity*—the crucial factor in any exercise program. Simply put, if you want to achieve a specific result, you need to design (and then follow) a specific training program. For example, the muscle-toning, body-shaping, and strength-training programs were specifically designed to use the proper load (percentage of 1RM or RMs) to cause the body to become more toned, more shaped, or stronger. Furthermore, when you selected an exercise for each muscle group or body area, you applied the principle of specificity: To train the chest muscles, you chose a chest exercise, not a leg exercise.

The weight training programs found in chapters 12 and 13 are more advanced than those found in part II because they are even more directly based on the specificity principle. Because a primary goal of a cross-training program (chapter 12) is to improve cardiovascular fitness, the program includes aerobic exercise, the type of exercise most helpful in reaching that goal. Similarly, chapter 13 guides you to choose specific exercises that mimic the movements found in the specific sport in which you want to enhance performance. For example, if you are a basketball player you understand the importance of jumping. To apply the principle of specificity, you need to select weight training exercises that are similar to jumping; if you do, your jumping ability will likely improve. Therefore, you would choose to perform the squat exercise rather than the leg extension or leg curl exercise. Although the leg extension and leg curl exercises train the leg muscles involved in jumping, the squat exercise mimics the actual jumping motion.

## CHAPTER 11

Design Your Own Program

So, let's say that you decide to design your own program. You may be in for a surprise because designing a weight training program can be challenging; more variables come into play than you probably realize. But to make this task easier, we have broken down the process into six simple steps. If you want to gain in-depth understanding of how to design your own program, consult the books listed in the reference section of this book.

After you've used one program for a period of time, you will find lifting the loads or completing the number of sets and repetitions prescribed in the program has become easier. This means that it's time to change your program so that you can continually make progress—not just plateau at one level. This chapter discusses how to increase your loads to spur improvement.

Step 1: Establish Goals for Weight Training

The first step in designing your own program is to determine your goals for training. Some commonly sought goals for weight training include increases in muscular endurance, size, strength, toning, and improvements in overall body shape or symmetry. What are your goals? Decide on them now. Recall, however, that the guidelines about training specificity described in part III mean that you should not choose weight training goals that conflict with one another. For example, if you want your whole body to become bigger and stronger, recall that the principle of specificity recommends that you do not follow a program geared toward both muscle strength and size. On the other hand, you may choose different goals for different parts of the body. For example, if you are a runner you may want upper-body strength but lower-body muscular endurance.

Step 2: Determine Training Frequency

Before you can choose your exercises, you need to decide how many days a week you will train. People who are ready for (and are already accustomed to) weight training more than three days a week will need to know how many days they'll work out so that they will know how to group the exercises they select in step 3. The number of days per week that you will weight train is based on your personal or work schedule, how well trained you are, and how many days you may be doing other forms of exercise (if you are cross-training, for instance).

©Sport the Library

Designing your own program allows you to customize the components to help you reach your goals.

Beginners should perform two or three workouts a week that are spaced out evenly (e.g., Monday and Thursday, or Monday, Wednesday, and Friday). After you have consistently followed a weight training program for at least several months, you may want to work out four days per week. In either case, be sure to spread out your workouts evenly throughout the week. That way, you will get the recovery you need between workouts, but too much time will not elapse between the days that you train. For example, a Monday and Wednesday schedule allows too much rest from the Wednesday workout to the following Monday.

If you are better trained you can handle more than three workouts per week, but with an odd number of days in a week you will have to weight train on consecutive days. A split routine includes four or more workouts equally spread out in a week (as in level 4 of chapter 8 or level 3 of chapter 9), but each workout consists of exercises that train only one part of the body (such as the upper body or the lower body). The result is that you are weight training more often but still have enough rest days between similar workouts.

Locate the appropriate workout chart in appendix A based on the number of days that you intend to train and use it to record your workouts.

Step 3: Select Exercises

After assessing your goals, you need to decide which exercises to include in your program. Keep in mind the principle of specificity when deciding which body parts you will emphasize in the program and what sport or activity you are training for (see chapter 13). If your special interest is chest and arm development, then you need to include exercises that stress those muscle areas. If you have already completed some of the programs in this book, you may have found a certain exercise that you do not like; if so, don't include it in your new program!

As you select each of your exercises, be sure to consider what equipment you need, which ones require a spotter, and how many you can complete in the time you have available to train. Then make a list of your exercises and determine if they involve free weights or pivot or cam machines. In addition, if you plan to follow a split routine you need to decide how you are going to group those exercises.

Step 4: Arrange Exercises

Decisions on how to arrange exercises are important because they affect the intensity of training. You can use several methods, such as exercising large muscle groups first (see table 11.1) or alternating upper- and lower-body exercises (table 11.2).

The most common arrangement is to alternate pushing exercises with pulling exercises. With this method, you would follow a push exercise (like the bench press) with a pull exercise (like the lat pulldown), or you might follow a pull exercise (like the biceps curl) with a push exercise (like the triceps pushdown). Table 11.3 provides an example of this push-pull exercise arrangement. No single method suits everyone; sometimes the equipment available will determine your arrangement decisions. Whatever order you select, try to avoid taxing the same muscle group repeatedly without allowing adequate time for recovery.

After you chose an arrangement method, write the names of the exercises you selected in step 3 into the workout chart that you located in step 2.

Table 11.1 Large to Small Muscle Group Arrangement

Exercise	Relative muscle size	Muscle group or body area
Lunge	Large	Thigh
Heel raise	Small	Calf
Bench press	Large	Chest
Lat pulldown	Large	Upper back
Triceps extension	Small	Back of the arm (triceps)
Biceps curl	Small	Front of the arm (biceps)

Adapted, by permission, from T.R. Baechle, B.R. Groves, 1998, *Weight training: steps to success,* 2nd ed. (Champaign, IL: Human Kinetics), 119.

Table 11.2 Alternating Upper-Body and Lower-Body Exercises

Exercise	Body location	Muscle group or body area
Bench press	Upper body	Chest
Lunge	Lower body	Thigh
Biceps curl	Upper body	Front of the arm (biceps)
Leg extension	Lower body	Front of the thigh (quadriceps)
Standing press	Upper body	Shoulder
Leg curl	Lower body	Back of the thigh (hamstrings)

Adapted, by permission, from T.R. Baechle, B.R. Groves, 1992, *Weight training: steps to success.* (Champaign, IL: Human Kinetics), 136.

Table 11.3 Alternating Push With Pull Exercises

Exercise	Type of exercise	Muscle group or body area
Leg press	Push	Thigh
Leg curl	Pull	Back of the thigh (hamstrings)
Heel raise	Push	Calf
Sit-up	Pull	Abdomen
Bench press	Push	Chest
Lat pulldown	Pull	Back
Seated press	Push	Shoulder
Biceps curl	Pull	Front of the arm (biceps)
Triceps extension	Push	Back of the arm (triceps)

Adapted, by permission, from T.R. Baechle, B.R. Groves, 1998, Weight training: steps to success, 2nd ed. (Champaign, IL: Human Kinetics), 119.

Step 5: Determine Loads, Sets, and Repetitions

After arranging your exercises in an appropriate order, you need to determine what loads to use for each exercise. This process, which was carefully detailed in chapter 5, will help you set the correct loads for your new program. Start light (lighter than you think you should start with!) and add weight as needed to allow you to complete the desired number of repetitions. An exciting characteristic of weight training is that you can vary the loads, the number of sets, and the number of repetitions to produce the changes that you want. Table 11.4 shows you how to achieve significant strength gains by using heavier loads with fewer repetitions (1 to 8) and performing three to five sets of the most important exercises. If you want muscle toning, you need to use lighter loads with many repetitions (12 to 20) and to include two to three sets of each exercise. This type of training program will also contribute to improvements in your cardio-vascular fitness if you integrate aerobic intervals with the weight training (as presented in chapter 12). If you want body shaping, you should use moderate loads with a moderate number of repetitions (8 to 12) and perform three to six sets. Combining a body-shaping weight training program with sensible eating and aerobic exercise workouts on other days of the week is an especially effective strategy for losing body fat and increasing muscle size (in men) or sculpting the body (in women)—with the result being attractive changes to your body.

Table 11.4 Three Outcomes of Weight Training Programs

Outcome of training	Relative loading	Repetition range	Number of sets	Rest between sets
Muscle toning	Light	12-20	2-3	20-30 seconds
Body shaping	Moderate	8-12	3-6	30-90 seconds
Strength training	Heavy	1-8	3-5	2-5 minutes

Adapted, by permission, from T.R. Baechle, B.R. Groves, 1998, *Weight training: steps to success,* 2nd ed. (Champaign, IL: Human Kinetics), 127.

Step 6: Determine Length of Rest Periods

Decide on the length of your rest periods between sets; the rest period will vary depending on your training goal. Table 11.4 shows you how to plan longer rest periods for strength development, moderate rest periods for body shaping, and short rest periods for muscle toning. If you are a beginner, be conservative; allow a little extra time between sets and exercises for the first several workouts so that you can gradually become accustomed to working out.

Making Continual Improvements

As your training level improves, you may want to modify, or "progress," your program by changing one or more of the variables discussed in this chapter. Experiment with different training approaches and find what works best for you. Although typically the more sets you perform of each exercise, the more or faster you will improve, the most important factor is to train within your ability—don't overdo it! Make your training decisions carefully, based on your fitness level, experience, and training goals.

You can apply progression to your program in many ways. You may wish to perform other (or more) exercises, train more often, order your exercises in a different way, or increase the number of sets that you perform in each exercise, the loads you use, or any combination of these changes. We've provided guidelines for choosing exercises, designing a split routine, and arranging exercises in a workout, but this section provides more explanation about when—and by how much—to increase training loads.

When to Increase Training Loads

Even after you've determined an appropriate training load, to make your strength continue to increase you will need to adjust your loads. How will you know when to make those changes? Two methods are available for you to use in determining when to increase training loads.

Two-for-Two Rule

A conservative method is to use the two-for-two rule. When you are able to perform two (or more) repetitions beyond the goal or desired number of repetitions in the last set—and then are able to repeat that performance for two consecutive workouts—you should increase the weight in that exercise for the next workout.

For example, if you are supposed to perform 15 reps for two sets in an exercise and you become strong enough over time to complete 17 reps in the second (last) set for two workout days in a row (like a Monday and the following Wednesday in a Monday, Wednesday, and Friday program), you should increase the load for the next workout.

Set-by-Set Method

A more progressive approach when completing more than one set for an exercise involves increasing the load based on how well you perform *each* set (rather than for *all* the sets as in the two-for-two rule). If you are supposed to do three sets of an exercise, follow a 2-1-3 guideline: When you are able to perform the goal number of repetitions in each set, increase the load in the second set first and complete subsequent workouts with that changed load in the second set. As soon as you are able to reach the goal reps in that second set, increase the load in the first set to match the load in the second set. Then, eventually, you will be able handle a load increase in the third set.

For an example, let's say that you can complete three sets of 10 reps with 100 pounds in the bench press exercise without a problem; the first change will be to increase the load for the second set. Your new workout becomes 100 pounds in set 1, 110 pounds in set 2, and 100 pounds in set 3. When you are able to complete the number of goal reps in all three sets again, you increase the load for the first set. Now you are lifting 110 pounds in set 1, 110 pounds in set 2, and 100 pounds in set 3. Over time, you will become stronger. When you can again meet the goal reps for all three sets, increase the load in the third set so that all three sets are at 110 pounds. Here are the strategies for other numbers of sets:

- For two sets, increase the load in the first set first and then the second set.
- For four sets, increase the load in the second set first, then the first set, then the third set, and finally the fourth set.

- For five sets, increase the load in the third set first, then the second set, then the first set, then the fourth set, and finally the fifth set.

How Much to Increase Training Loads

You now know when to make load increases, but how big should the increase be? Recall that chapter 5 explained that exercises that involve large muscle groups, such as the chest, shoulders, and thighs and hips are referred to as *core* exercises. These muscles can handle heavier loads and larger load increases than the smaller muscle groups can, like those found in the forearms, arms, neck, or calves, which you train using noncore exercises. Thus, you will first need to determine the type of exercise for which you want to make load increases. Then, based on the body area and your training status (your level number if you are following a program from chapters 7 through 9 *or* a description of how well trained you think you are), consult table 11.5 to see how much you should increase the load.

These guidelines can help you determine how much to increase the load for an exercise in your program, but realize that they won't work for everyone for every exercise. If the increased load is too heavy, return to the lighter load, use it in your workouts for a few more weeks, and then try to increase the load again. Often, it is a trial-and-error process, not an exact science.

Table 11.5 Increasing Training Loads

Training level or description	DESCRIPTION OF THE EXERCISE		Load increase
	Body area	Type	
Levels 1-2: beginner	Upper body	Core	2.5-5 pounds (1-2 kg)
	Upper body	Noncore	1.25-2.5 pounds (0.6-1 kg)
	Lower body	Core	10-15 pounds (4-7 kg)
	Lower body	Noncore	5-10 pounds (2-4 kg)
Levels 3-6: intermediate or advanced	Upper body	Core	5-10+ pounds (2-4+ kg)
	Upper body	Noncore	5-10 pounds (2-4 kg)
	Lower body	Core	15-50+ pounds (7-23+ kg)
	Lower body	Noncore	10-15 pounds (4-7 kg)

Adapted, by permission, from R.W. Earle, T.R. Baechle, 2004, *NSCA's essentials of personal training*, (Champaign, IL: Human Kinetics), 383.

## CHAPTER 12

Combine Weight Training With Aerobic Exercise

After following your weight training program for several months, you may become bored with it. Rather than stop your training, consider a cross training program. Recall from chapter 1 that although weight training can improve the fitness components of muscular strength, muscular endurance, body composition, and flexibility, its value in promoting cardiovascular fitness is minimal. By adding aerobic exercise to your weight training workouts, you can add variety while improving your cardiovascular fitness level. The cross-training programs that follow will help you continue to enjoy the gains made from your weight training program while you improve your cardiovascular fitness and overall appearance.

Cross-Training for the Muscle-Toning Program

To add cross-training workouts to your muscle-toning program, include an aerobic exercise "interval" after every weight training set. The aerobic interval should consist of stair climbing, stationary cycling, jogging in place, jumping rope, or any other type of aerobic exercise that you can perform near the weight training exercise stations. The length of each aerobic exercise interval can be 30 to 60 seconds.

After the last repetition of each weight training set, begin immediately performing whatever aerobic exercise you have filled in on your workout chart (it helps to have the machine set up so that it is ready for you to begin immediately after your set). To maximize the benefits of a cross-training program, do not delay the start of the aerobic interval. Then, when the 30- to 60-second aerobic interval ends (decide in advance how long it will be), take your exercise heart rate (see the section "Determining the Intensity of the Aerobic Component" to learn how to do this).

Cross-Training for the Body-Shaping Program

To add cross-training to your body-shaping program, add an aerobic workout on the days that you do not weight train; you will be exercising a total of four to six days per week. Although the body-shaping workouts will develop your muscles and shape your body, adding aerobic exercise to your overall program will more quickly bring about a sculpting effect to your body! Because aerobic exercise increases the number of calories that you burn, adding an aerobic workout to your overall program will reduce your body fat while the weight training builds up your muscles. The result of cross-training is a visually appealing physique. Many people choose to stair climb, stationary cycle, jog, run, walk, swim, or do an aerobic dance class two to three times per week on their days off from weight training. You should consider your weight training level when choosing the number of aerobic exercise sessions to complete each week. If you are a beginner following the level 1 or 2 workouts, add two days of aerobic exercise per week. If you are an intermediate exerciser and use the level 3 or 4 body-shaping workouts, you can do aerobic exercise three days per week. If you are more advanced and adhere to the level 5 or 6 workouts, you can also add three aerobic sessions per week. You will not need a special cross-training and weight training workout sheet, but you may want to record the time, distance, type of exercise, and exercise heart rate on a separate sheet or notebook to monitor your improvement.

Cross-Training for the Strength-Training Program

If you are serious about developing high levels of strength, you should not add aerobic exercise to a strength-training program. Because of the heavier loads required to improve muscular strength, you need to rest properly; this applies not only to the period between sets and exercises but to the nonweight training days as well. If you attempt to incorporate aerobic exercise into a strength-training program, you will find that you may not feel recovered or rested enough to complete the more intense weight training workouts; similarly, you may have to struggle through your aerobic workouts.

Determining the Intensity of the Aerobic Component

To determine the intensity of an aerobic exercise interval or workout, use your pulse or heart rate as a guide. The faster you cycle, jog, run, walk, or swim, the higher your heart rate will be. You should keep an eye on your heart rate during aerobic exercise so that you can determine whether you are exercising at a safe level yet exercising hard enough to improve your cardiovascular fitness. To determine your appropriate aerobic exercise intensity, follow these steps:

1. Determine your maximum heart rate (MHR).

   Subtract your age from 220:

   $$220 - \text{your age} = \text{MHR (beats per minute)}$$

   $220 -$ _____ (your age) = _____ your MHR

2. Determine your target heart rate (THR)

   Your heart rate should fall within a range of 70 to 85 percent of your MHR. So, multiply your MHR by 0.70 and 0.85 to determine your THR range in beats per minute:

   $$\text{MHR} \times 0.70 = \text{THR (lowest value)}$$

   _____ (your MHR) $\times$ 0.70 = _____ lowest THR

   $$\text{MHR} \times 0.85 = \text{THR (highest value)}$$

   _____ (your MHR) $\times$ 0.85 = _____ highest THR

For example, if you are 40 years old, your MHR is 180 beats per minute:

$$220 - 40 = 180$$

Your target heart rate range is 126 to 153 beats per minute:

$$180 \times 0.70 = 126 \text{ (lower limit)}$$

$$180 \times 0.85 = 153 \text{ (upper limit)}$$

For a quick and accurate assessment of your heart rate immediately after your aerobic exercise interval (for cross-training for the muscle-toning program) or during your aerobic exercise workout (for cross-training for the body-shaping program), count your pulse for 15 seconds and then multiply by 4 or refer to table 12.1. Thus, a 40-year-old's THR for a 15-second count would be the following:

126 beats per minute (lower limit) = about 31 beats per 15 seconds

153 beats per minute (upper limit) = about 38 beats per 15 seconds

To take your heart rate, you can feel, or palpate, your pulse on several places on your body. The most effective locations are at the radial artery on the thumb side of your wrist and at the carotid artery just below your jaw and down from your ear on your neck (see figure 12.1).

Immediately at the end of each aerobic interval or during your aerobic workout, simply look at your wristwatch or a wall clock, place your fingers at either pulse rate location, and count your heart rate for 15 seconds. Your goal is to reach but not exceed your 15-second THR range. If your

Table 12.1 Heart Rate Conversion Table

Heart rate (per minute)	Pulse rate (in 15 seconds)	Heart rate (per minute)	Pulse rate (in 15 seconds)
192	48	136	34
188	47	132	33
184	46	128	32
180	45	124	31
176	44	120	30
172	43	116	29
168	42	112	28
164	41	108	27
160	40	104	26
156	39	100	25
152	38	96	24
148	37	92	23
144	36	88	22
140	35		

For example, if you felt 38 heartbeats in 15 seconds, your heart rate per minute would be 152.

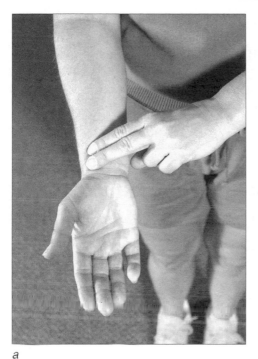 

a   b

Figure 12.1 Two places or techniques to feel a pulse are (a) at the radial artery on the wrist and (b) at the carotid artery on the neck.

pulse rate is too high, then step, pedal, jog, or jump rope more slowly. If your pulse is too low, increase your intensity.

When starting a program of cross-training for muscle toning, be aware that your exercise heart rate may not have time to get up to your THR from the aerobic interval, especially if the interval is only 30 seconds long or if it takes you time to get the aerobic machine going at the right speed. As you become in better shape, gain more familiarity with the equipment, and become accustomed to making the cross-training transition, you will be able to make the aerobic interval more demanding. The result will be continued improvement in cardiovascular fitness.

Setting the Duration of the Aerobic Component

For the muscle-toning program, the duration of your aerobic portion is the rest period between your weight training sets (approximately 30 to 60 seconds). When following a body-shaping cross-training program, the duration is longer. Beginners can perform 10 to 25 minutes of aerobic exercise per session. Intermediates can aerobically exercise 25 to 35 minutes, and advanced persons can complete 35 to 45 minutes of aerobic exercise per session. Be aware that these are only guidelines; for example, if you are in level 3, you do not have to run for 30 minutes each workout, especially if you have never run that far before. If you feel that the aerobic workouts are too difficult, move back to a lower level (i.e., use a lower percentage of your MHR, shorten the length of the aerobic workout, or both), and then make increases gradually. You will be more likely to stick to your cross-training program if you enjoy it and train at appropriate intensity and duration.

Fill in Your Cross-Training Workout Chart

If you plan to cross-train for the muscle-toning program, use a cross-training workout chart in appendix A to merge aerobic activity intervals with your weight training program. Remember, all the exercises, their numbers of sets and repetitions, and the number of workouts per week remain as shown in the workout levels. Follow the two steps outlined in chapter 5 but also fill in your choice of aerobic exercise or exercises on the cross-training workout chart:

1. Determine your THR range and write it in the space at the bottom of the chart.
2. Write in the name of an appropriate type of aerobic exercise in the space marked "aerobic exercise."
3. Take your heart rate immediately after completing the last aerobic interval and write it on the workout sheet.

## CHAPTER 13

Weight Training for a Sport

Many people who follow a weight training program participate regularly in a favorite sport or activity. Besides performing weight training to become more toned, shaped, or stronger, you can design an advanced program specifically geared to enhancing performance in your sport. The secret of an effective weight training program for a sport or activity lies in the application of the specificity principle. The more similar the weight training exercises are to the movements of the sport, the more beneficial those exercises are in improving performance.

If you want to develop an even more sport-specific weight training program—one that also considers the amount of load lifted and the number of reps performed—consult the reference books listed in the back of this book or hire a personal trainer who has experience and professional credentials to train and condition athletes.

Evaluate Your Sport

To apply the principle of specificity, you need to look at the primary or important movements involved in your sport. Observe how your whole body (especially your arms and legs) moves; if you can't visualize yourself,

©William J. Crane

To create a sport-specific weight training program, first assess your sport and identify how your body moves, then choose exercises that use the same movement patterns.

have a friend videotape you or watch the sport live or on television. You are looking for repetitive motions that are part of the important skills of the sport. To continue the example provided at the end of part III (see page 190), the sport of basketball further involves dribbling, passing, and shooting. In each movement, you are repeatedly extending (straightening) your elbow against resistance (the ball), with your upper arm next to your torso (to dribble), in front of your torso (to pass), or above the shoulders (to shoot). Thus, a sport-specific weight training program for basketball should include exercises that mimic some or all of these movements.

Choose Sport-Specific Exercises

Once you've identified the major movements of your sport, the true challenge is to find weight training exercises to match them. You must choose these exercises accurately. Many exercises appear to be similar in how the body moves (like the biceps curl on page 148 and the triceps pushdown on page 145; both involve nearly the same body position and movement at the elbow), but the muscles that cause those movements may be different (the biceps curl trains the muscle on the front of your upper arm, and the triceps extension trains the muscle on the back of your upper arm).

To simplify the process, look up your sport and its primary movements in table 13.1. For example, look at the back-of-the-arm (triceps) exercises listed for basketball and refer to the descriptions and photos of their proper technique provided in chapter 10. Despite the large variety of sports, most involve jumping, running, throwing, or hitting, so several "universal" exercises appear throughout the table. Also, be aware that although the table includes many sport movements, not every important or skill-related motion is listed because there are too many. The purpose of table 13.1 is to identify the basic sport movements and associate them with the exercises described in this book.

For example, if you observe the positions of the upper arm and the motion at the elbow, you'll notice that the triceps pushdown exercise is similar to dribbling the ball, the lying triceps extension exercise is somewhat like what the arms do during a chest pass, and the dumbbell triceps extension exercise matches the arm movement during a free-throw shot. Your program does not need to include all three of these exercises for the triceps (unless you are a well-trained, advanced athlete); selecting even one will make your weight training program more specific to basketball.

Table 13.1 Effective Weight Training Exercises for Various Sports

Sport	Primary movements	Sport-specific weight training exercises
American football Hockey Rugby	Agility-type sprinting Blocking Tackling	Power clean (FW) Squat (FW); squat (RB); lunge (FW) Bench press (FW); bench press (PM); chest press (CM); chest press (RB) Standing shoulder press (FW); seated press (PM); shoulder press (CM); shoulder press (RB) Biceps curl (FW); low pulley biceps curl (PM); machine biceps curl (CM); biceps curl (RB) Dumbbell triceps extension (FW); triceps pushdown (PM); triceps extension (CM); one-arm triceps extension (RB)
Archery	Pulling	Bent-over row (FW); one-arm dumbbell row (FW); seated row (PM); seated row (RB) Biceps curl (FW); low pulley biceps curl (PM); machine biceps curl (CM); biceps curl (RB)
Badminton Racquetball Squash Table tennis Tennis	Racquet serve Racquet stroke	Power clean (FW) Lunge (FW) Machine pullover (CM) Dumbbell fly (FW); pec deck (CM) Bench press (FW); bench press (PM); chest press (CM); chest press (RB) Dumbbell lateral raise (FW); lateral raise (RB) Dumbbell triceps extension (FW); triceps pushdown (PM); triceps extension (CM); one-arm triceps extension (RB) Sit-up (FW); abdominal crunch (CM)

(continued)

Table 13.1 *(continued)*

Sport	Primary movements	Sport-specific weight training exercises
Baseball Softball	Throwing Batting Sprinting	Power clean (FW) Squat (FW); squat (RB); lunge (FW) Machine pullover (CM) Lying triceps extension (FW); triceps pushdown (PM); triceps extension (CM); one-arm triceps extension (RB) Dumbbell fly (FW); pec deck (CM) Dumbbell lateral raise (FW); lateral raise (RB) Sit-up (FW); abdominal crunch (CM)
Basketball	Jumping Dribbling Passing Shooting	Power clean (FW) Squat (FW); squat (RB); lunge (FW) Angled leg press (FW); leg press (PM); horizontal leg press (CM) Standing heel raise (FW); standing heel raise (PM); seated heel raise (PM) Dumbbell triceps extension (FW); triceps push-down (PM); lying triceps extension (FW); one-arm triceps extension (RB) Standing shoulder press (FW); seated press (PM); shoulder press (CM); shoulder press (RB) Bench press (FW); bench press (PM); chest press (CM); chest press (RB)
Bowling	Backswing Follow-through	Dumbbell triceps extension (FW); triceps push-down (PM); triceps extension (CM); one-arm triceps extension (RB) Biceps curl (FW); low pulley biceps curl (PM); machine biceps curl (CM); biceps curl (RB) Bench press (FW); bench press (PM); chest press (CM); chest press (RB) Lunge (FW) Leg (knee) curl (CM) Leg (knee) extension (CM)
Boxing	Punching	Bench press (FW); bench press (PM); chest press (CM); chest press (RB) Dumbbell triceps extension (FW); triceps push-down (PM); triceps extension (CM); one-arm triceps extension (RB) Standing shoulder press (FW); seated press (PM); shoulder press (CM); shoulder press (RB) Dumbbell fly (FW); pec deck (CM) Machine pullover (CM)

Sport	Primary movements	Sport-specific weight training exercises
Crew	Rowing (upper body) Pushing (lower body)	Bent over row (FW); one-arm dumbbell row (FW); seated row (PM); seated row (RB) Angled leg press (FW); leg press (PM); horizontal leg press (CM) Power clean (FW) Squat (FW); squat (RB) Leg (knee) extension (CM)
Cross country running/ skiing	Forward-type running	Lunge (FW) Leg (knee) curl (CM) Leg (knee) extension (CM) Bent-over row (FW); one-arm dumbbell row (FW); seated row (PM); seated row (RB) Biceps curl (FW); low pulley biceps curl (PM); machine biceps curl (CM); biceps curl (RB) Dumbbell triceps extension (FW); triceps push-down (PM); triceps extension (CM); one-arm triceps extension (RB)
Cycling	Pedal stroke	Lunge (FW) Leg (knee) curl (CM) Leg (knee) extension (CM) Standing heel raise (FW); standing heel raise (PM); seated heel raise (PM)
Golf	Backswing Follow-through (upper body)	Bent-over row (FW); one-arm dumbbell row (FW); seated row (PM); seated row (RB) Dumbbell fly (FW); pec deck (CM) Bench press (FW); bench press (PM); chest press (CM); chest press (RB) Dumbbell triceps extension (FW); triceps push-down (PM); triceps extension (CM); one-arm triceps extension (RB) Sit-up (FW); abdominal crunch (CM)
Gymnastics	Tumbling Jumping Bar exercise	Power clean (FW) Squat (FW); squat (RB); lunge (FW) Bench press (FW); bench press (PM); chest press (CM); chest press (RB) Bent-over row (FW); one-arm dumbbell row (FW); seated row (PM); seated row (RB) Biceps curl (FW); low pulley biceps curl (PM); machine biceps curl (CM); biceps curl (RB) Dumbbell triceps extension (FW); triceps push-down (PM); triceps extension (CM); one-arm triceps extension (RB) Standing shoulder press (FW); seated press (PM); shoulder press (CM); shoulder press (RB) Lat pulldown (PM)

(continued)

Table 13.1 *(continued)*

Sport	Primary movements	Sport-specific weight training exercises
Lacrosse Soccer	Kicking Jumping Agility-type sprinting	Power clean (FW) Squat (FW); squat (RB); lunge (FW) Leg (knee) curl (CM) Leg (knee) extension (CM)
Martial arts	Punching Kicking Blocking	Dumbbell triceps extension (FW); triceps push-down (PM); triceps extension (CM); one-arm triceps extension (RB) Machine pullover (CM) Leg (knee) curl (CM) Leg (knee) extension (CM) Squat (FW); squat (RB)
Skate-boarding Snow-boarding Surfing Waterskiing	Balancing (in a semi-squat position)	Squat (FW); squat (RB); lunge (FW) Leg (knee) curl (CM) Leg (knee) extension (CM) Standing heel raise (FW); standing heel raise (PM); seated heel raise (PM)
Skating (any type)	Lunging Stroking	Lunge (FW) Squat (FW); squat (RB) Angled leg press (FW); leg press (PM); horizontal leg press (CM) Standing heel raise (FW); standing heel raise (PM); seated heel raise (PM) Leg (knee) curl (CM) Leg (knee) extension (CM)
Swimming	Stroke swimming	Lat pulldown (PM); Machine pullover (CM); Dumbbell fly (FW); pec deck (CM) Bench press (FW); bench press (PM); chest press (CM); chest press (RB) Dumbbell lateral raise (FW); lateral raise (RB) Dumbbell triceps extension (FW); triceps push-down (PM); triceps extension (CM); one-arm triceps extension (RB) Sit-up (FW); abdominal crunch (CM)

Sport	Primary movements	Sport-specific weight training exercises
(Track and) Field events	Jumping Throwing Sprinting	Power clean (FW) Lunge (FW) Squat (FW); squat (RB) Machine pullover (CM) Dumbbell triceps extension (FW); triceps push-down (PM); triceps extension (CM); one-arm triceps extension (RB) Dumbbell fly (FW); pec deck (CM) Dumbbell lateral raise (FW); lateral raise (RB)
Volleyball	Jumping Ball blocking Ball serving Lunging	Power clean (FW) Squat (FW); squat (RB); lunge (FW) Standing heel raise (FW); standing heel raise (PM); seated heel raise (PM) Standing shoulder press (FW); seated press (PM); shoulder press (CM); shoulder press (RB) Dumbbell lateral raise (FW); lateral raise (RB) Machine pullover (CM) Dumbbell triceps extension (FW); triceps push-down (PM); triceps extension (CM); one-arm triceps extension (RB)
Walking	Walking	Lunge (FW) Leg (knee) curl (CM) Leg (knee) extension (CM) Standing heel raise (FW); standing heel raise (PM)
Wrestling	Takedown Grapping	Power clean (FW) Squat (FW); squat (RB) Bench press (FW); bench press (PM); chest press (CM); chest press (RB) Standing shoulder press (FW); seated press (PM); shoulder press (CM); shoulder press (RB) Lat pulldown (PM) Bent-over row (FW); seated row Dumbbell triceps extension (FW); triceps push-down (PM); triceps extension (CM); one-arm triceps extension (RB) Biceps curl (FW); low pulley biceps curl (PM); machine (preacher) biceps curl (CM); biceps curl (RB) Sit-up (FW); abdominal crunch (CM)

Free weight (FW), pivot machine (PM), cam machine (CM), and resistance band (RB). Nearly all of the exercises listed are found in this book; go to chapter 10 to learn their proper technique.

Insert Sport-Specific Exercises Into Your Program

After following the guidelines detailed in chapters 3 and 4 to check your weight training fitness status, choose your desired training goal, and determine your initial training level, you are ready to develop a program that is (more) specific to your favorite sport or activity. Although a person following a general weight training program completes both steps as described in chapter 5, you will take a detour. After locating the workout in chapters 7 through 9 (or even in chapter 12), making a copy of the appropriate workout chart from appendix A, and choosing the days that you'll train, you will replace (or add) the exercises listed for that workout with those listed for your sport in table 13.1. Be sure that you exchange exercises with those that train the same muscle group or body area so that your program will still be balanced and affect your whole body. The recommendations in the section "Select and Record Exercises" of step 1 are still suitable; you will just be performing exercises specifically geared to improving your sport performance.

Clarification for Workout Level 1 Programs

The exercises included in all level 1 programs were selected because they have known coefficients to multiply by a person's body weight to establish starting loads (see chapter 5). To follow a level 1 program, you may not be able to make as many sport-specific exercise substitutions. The exercises listed in table 13.1 do not all appear in tables 5.2 and 5.3 (load calculation tables for women and men) on pages 30-32. The best guideline is to follow the level 1 program as listed and then modify your program to be more sport specific when you progress to level 2.

Reminder About Workout Level 2 Through 6 Programs

When you substitute sport-specific exercises in your program, it is possible that you will replace a core exercise with a noncore exercise (or vice versa). To minimize injury caused by overloading noncore exercises or to maximize the benefit of more heavily loading core exercises, be aware of which exercises are core and which are noncore (see table 5.7 on page 34). Observing this distinction will allow you to follow the guidelines in step 2 of chapter 5 to determine training loads.

You will be amazed how a program specifically designed for your sport will improve your performance.

Appendix

Weight Training Two Days Per Week

#	Exercises	Sets/ Reps	Set	Day 1			Day 2		
				1	2	3	1	2	3
1			Wt.						
			Reps						
2			Wt.						
			Reps						
3			Wt.						
			Reps						
4			Wt.						
			Reps						
5			Wt.						
			Reps						
6			Wt.						
			Reps						
7			Wt.						
			Reps						

Zone_____ Week _____ Comments _____

Date_____

From *Fitness Weight Training, Second Edition* by Thomas R. Baechle and Roger W. Earle, 2005, Champaign, IL: Human Kinetics.

Weight Training Three Days Per Week

#	Exercises	Sets/ Reps	Set	Day 1 1	Day 1 2	Day 1 3	Day 1 4	Day 2 1	Day 2 2	Day 2 3	Day 2 4	Day 3 1	Day 3 2	Day 3 3	Day 3 4
1			Wt.												
			Reps												
2			Wt.												
			Reps												
3			Wt.												
			Reps												
4			Wt.												
			Reps												
5			Wt.												
			Reps												
6			Wt.												
			Reps												
7			Wt.												
			Reps												
8			Wt.												
			Reps												
9			Wt.												
			Reps												
10			Wt.												
			Reps												

Zone_____Week_____

Date_____

Comments_____

_____

_____

From *Fitness Weight Training, Second Edition* by Thomas R. Baechle and Roger W. Earle, 2005, Champaign, IL: Human Kinetics.

Weight Training Four Days Per Week

#	Upper-body exercises	Sets/ Reps	Set	Day 1 1	2	3	4	Day 3 1	2	3	4
1			Wt.								
			Reps								
2			Wt.								
			Reps								
3			Wt.								
			Reps								
4			Wt.								
			Reps								
5			Wt.								
			Reps								
6			Wt.								
			Reps								
7			Wt.								
			Reps								

#	Lower-body exercise	Sets/ Reps	Set	Day 2 1	2	3	4	Day 4 1	2	3	4
1			Wt.								
			Reps								
2			Wt.								
			Reps								
3			Wt.								
			Reps								
4			Wt.								
			Reps								
5			Wt.								
			Reps								
6			Wt.								
			Reps								

Zone_____ Week_____

Date _____

Comments_____
_____
_____

From *Fitness Weight Training, Second Edition* by Thomas R. Baechle and Roger W. Earle, 2005, Champaign, IL: Human Kinetics.

Cross-Training Three Days Per Week

#	Exercises	Sets/ Reps	Set	Day 1				Day 2				Day 3			
				1	2	3	4	1	2	3	4	1	2	3	4
1			Wt.												
			Reps												
2			Wt.												
			Reps												
3			Wt.												
			Reps												
4			Wt.												
			Reps												
5			Wt.												
			Reps												
6			Wt.												
			Reps												
7			Wt.												
			Reps												
8			Wt.												
			Reps												
9			Wt.												
			Reps												
10			Wt.												
			Reps												

Zone_____Week_____
Date_____

THR range_____
_____
HR _____

Aerobic exercise_____
_____
_____

From *Fitness Weight Training, Second Edition* by Thomas R. Baechle and Roger W. Earle, 2005, Champaign, IL: Human Kinetics.

Cross-Training Four Days Per Week

#	Upper-body exercises	Sets/ Reps	Set	Day 1				Day 3			
				1	2	3	4	1	2	3	4
1			Wt.								
			Reps								
2			Wt.								
			Reps								
3			Wt.								
			Reps								
4			Wt.								
			Reps								
5			Wt.								
			Reps								
6			Wt.								
			Reps								
7			Wt.								
			Reps								

#	Lower-body exercise	Sets/ Reps	Set	Day 2				Day 4			
				1	2	3	4	1	2	3	4
1			Wt.								
			Reps								
2			Wt.								
			Reps								
3			Wt.								
			Reps								
4			Wt.								
			Reps								
5			Wt.								
			Reps								
6			Wt.								
			Reps								

Zone_____ Week_____

Date _____

THR range_____

HR _____

Aerobic exercise_____

From *Fitness Weight Training, Second Edition* by Thomas R. Baechle and Roger W. Earle, 2005, Champaign, IL: Human Kinetics.

References

Baechle, T.R., and B.R. Groves. 1994. *Weight Training Instruction.* Champaign, IL: Human Kinetics.

Baechle, T.R., and B.R. Groves. 1998. *Weight Training: Steps to Success.* 2nd edition. Champaign, IL: Human Kinetics.

Baechle, T.R., and B.R. Groves. 1993. *Weight Training Video.* Champaign, IL: Human Kinetics.

Baechle, T.R., and R.W. Earle, eds. 2000. *Essentials of Strength Training and Conditioning.* 2nd edition. Champaign, IL: Human Kinetics.

Clark, N. 2003. *Nancy Clark's Sports Nutrition Guidebook.* 3rd edition. Champaign, IL: Human Kinetics.

Earle, R.W., and T.R. Baechle, eds. 2004. *NSCA's Essentials of Personal Training.* Champaign, IL: Human Kinetics.

Faigenbaum, A., and W. Westcott. 2000. *Strength and Power for Young Athletes.* Champaign, IL: Human Kinetics.

Westcott, W., and T.R. Baechle. 1999. *Strength Training for Seniors.* Champaign, IL: Human Kinetics.

Westcott, W., and T.R. Baechle. 1998. *Strength Training Past 50.* Champaign, IL: Human Kinetics.

Williams, M.H. 1999. *Nutrition for Health, Fitness, and Sport.* 5th edition. Boston, MA: McGraw-Hill Publishers.

Willmore, J.R., and D.L. Costill. 2004. *Physiology of Sport and Exercise.* 3rd edition. Champaign, IL: Human Kinetics.

Index

Note: The italicized *f* and *t* following page numbers refer to figures and tables, respectively.

A

abdominal exercises
   abdominal crunch (PM, CM) 142
   sit-up (FW) 141
aerobic component, intensity of
   determining 201-202
   heart rate conversion table 202, 202*t*
   taking heart rate 202, 203, 203*f*
aerobic component, setting duration of
   203-204
aerobic exercise
   advantages and disadvantages 4-5
   compared with weight training 5
   rapid results 5
   weight training, benefits of 5
attire for weight training
   gloves 14
   men and women 13-14
   shoes 14
   weight belts 14
   what not to wear 14

B

back exercises
   bent-over row (FW) 153
   lat pulldown (PM, CM) 156
   machine pullover (CM) 157
   one-arm dumbbell row (FW) 154
   seated row (PM, CM) 155
   seated row (RB) 158
back of arms (triceps) exercises
   dumbbell triceps extension (FW) 143
   lying triceps extension (FW) 144
   one-arm triceps extension (RB) 147

   triceps extension (CM) 146
   triceps pushdown (PM) 145
back of thigh (hamstrings) exercises, leg
   (knee) curl (PM, CM) 177-178
barbell lifting technique 41-42, 42*f*
barbell lowering technique 43
barbells
   cambered or curl bars 12
   description of 12, 13*f*
   Olympic bars 12, 13*f*
   Olympic weight plates 12, 13*f*
   outside collars (locks) 12, 13*f*
   safety considerations 12
   standard and cambered bars 12, 13*f*
   weight plates 12, 13*f*
bench press test 20-21, 21*t*
biceps exercises. *See* front of arms (biceps)
   exercises
body shaping
   description of 4, 75-103
   girth changes 4
   workouts 77-103
breathing correctly 43-44

C

calves, exercises for
   seated heel raise (PM) 160
   standing heel raise (FW) 159
   standing heel raise (PM) 160
cam machines (CM)
   description of 11
   example 11*f*
   safety considerations 11

chest exercises
    bench press (FW) 162
    bench press (PM) 164-165
    chest press (CM) 166
    chest press (RB) 168
    dumbbell fly (FW) 163-164
    pec deck (PM, CM) 167
Clark, Nancy 26
cross-country skiing 5
cross-training
    for body-shaping program 200
    for muscle-toning program 199-200
    for strength-training program 200-201
    workout chart 204
cycling 5

D
dumbbells
    description of 12
    example 13*f*
    safety considerations 12

E
elastic cable 9
equipment
    types of weight training equipment 9-13
    weight training attire 13-14
    weight training facilities 15-16

F
facilities
    training at fitness facility 16
    training at home 15
fitness facility
    training without personal trainer 16
    training with personal trainer 16
fixed-resistance pivot machines 10
free weights. *See also* training precautions
    barbells 12, 13*f*
    dumbbells 12, 13
    free-weight exercise, description of 12
    safety considerations for 12
front of arms (biceps) exercises
    biceps curl (FW) 148
    biceps curl (RB) 152
    dumbbell biceps curl (FW) 149
    low pulley curl (PM) 150
    preacher curl (CM) 151
front of thigh (quadriceps) exercises, leg
    (knee) extension (PM, CM) 179

G
gloves for weight training 14
grips 39-40, 40*f*, 41, 41*f*

H
home facility
    basic equipment requirements 9, 15
    room location and design 15

I
improvements, continual
    progression to program, applying 196
    training loads, how much to increase
        198, 198*t*
    training loads, when to increase 197-
        198
initial training level 24, 24*t*, 25

J
jogging 4, 5

L
lifting fundamentals
    breathing correctly 43-44
    grips 39-40, 40*f*, 41, 41*f*
    lifting bar 41-42, 42*f*
    lowering bar 43
    weight belt 43
load guidelines (level 1)
    calculating trial load, example 32, 33*t*
    load adjustment table 32, 33, 33*t*
    load calculation table for men 30, 30*t*-31*t*
    load calculation table for women 30,
        30*t*-31*t*
    making load adjustments (level 1) 32
    steps for establishing 30
    trial load 32
    using load adjustment table, example
        33, 33*t*
load guidelines (level 2 through 6)
    determining training loads 35, 36*t*-37*t*
    making load adjustments 37-38, 38*t*
    1RM procedure for core exercises 34,
        34*t*, 35
    training loads for core exercises, deter-
        mining 35, 35*t*
    training loads for noncore exercises 37,
        37*t*

M
machines. *See also* training precautions
    cam machines (CM) 11, 11*f*
    machine exercises, description 10
    pivot machines (PM) 10, 10*f*
    safety considerations for 11
muscles
    front view 6*f*
    rear view 7*f*

muscle toning
  description of 4
  workouts 57-74

N

Nancy Clark's Sports Nutrition Guidebook
    26

P

(PAR-Q) Physical Activity Readiness Questionnaire 18-19
personal trainer, training with and without 16
pivot machines (PM)
  description of 10
  fixed-resistance pivot machines 10
  safety-considerations 11
  single-unit 10, 10f
  variable-resistance pivot machines 10
program, designing your own
  improvements, continual 196-198, 198t
  specificity principle 190
  step 1: goals for weight training 191-192
  step 2: training frequency 192-193
  step 3: selecting exercises 193
  step 4: arranging exercises 193-194, 194t, 195t
  step 5: determining loads, sets, and repetitions 195, 196t
  step 6: determining length of rest periods 196, 196t
program, setting up
  step 1: fill in workout chart 27-28, 29t, 30
  step 2: determining training loads 29, 30, 30t-38t, 32-35, 37-38
program, starting
  initial training level 24, 24t, 25
  keys of effective training 25-26
  my weight training program 25
  training goal, choosing 23-24

R

resistance bands
  exercising with 13
  safety considerations 13
rubber tubing 9

S

set-by-set method 197-198
shoes for weight training 14
shoulder exercises
  dumbbell lateral raise (FW) 182

lateral raise (RB) 185
seated (or shoulder) press (PM, CM) 183
shoulder press (RB) 184
standing press (FW) 180-181
single-unit machine 10, 10f
sport-specific exercises, inserting into program
  clarification for workout level 1 programs 30t-32t, 207t-211t, 212
  workout level 2 though 6 programs, reminder 34t, 212
strength training
  strength 4
  strength increases 4
  strength training programs 4
  workouts 108-137
stretching exercises
  back and hips 48
  calves 50
  chest and shoulders 47
  hamstrings and lower back 49
  precautions 46
  quadriceps 49
  upper back, shoulders, and back of arms 47
  upper back and back of arms 48
swimming 5

T

testing weight training fitness
  bench press test 20-21
  benefits of 17
  muscular fitness norms of bench press test 21, 21t
  (PAR-Q) Physical Activity Readiness Questionnaire 18-19
thigh exercises
  angled leg press (FW) 172-173
  horizontal leg press (PM, CM) 174-175
  leg press (PM) 174
  lunge (FW) 171-172
  squat (FW) 169-170
  squat (RB) 176
training, effective
  increasing workout intensity gradually 25
  nutrition and rest 26
  positive attitude 26
  training regularly 25
training at fitness facility
  training without personal trainer 16
  training with personal trainer 16

training at home
    basic equipment requirements 15
    room location and design 15
training goal
    choosing 23-24
    for program 23-24
training loads, determining
    level 1 load guidelines 30-33, 30*t*-32*t*, 33*t*
    level 2 through 6 load guidelines 34, 34*t*,
       35, 35*t*, 36*t*-37*t*, 37-38, 38*t*
    level to use 29
training precautions
    using free weights 44-45
    using machines 45
triceps exercises. *See* back of arms (triceps) exercises
two-for-two rule 197

V
variable-resistance pivot machines 10

W
walking 4, 5
warm up and cool down 45-50. *See also*
    stretching exercises
    cool down 50
    importance of 45-46
    stretching exercises 46-50
    warm up 46
weight belt(s)
    description of 14
    when to wear 43
weight plates 12, 13*f*
weight train for fitness
    aerobic exercise *versus* weight training
      4-5
    body shaping 4
    matching individual goals with outcomes 3
    muscles, front and rear views 5, 6*f*, 7*f*
    muscle toning 4
    strength training 4
    workouts, types 3
weight training
    advantages of 1
    compared with aerobic activities 5
    quality of life 1
weight training equipment, types
    free weights 9, 12, 13, 13*f*
    machines 9, 10, 10*f*, 11, 11*f*
    resistance bands 9, 13
weight training exercises
    abdomen 140-142
    arrangement of exercises 139

    back 153-158
    back of arms (triceps) 143-147
    back of thigh (hamstrings) 177-178
    calves 159-161
    chest 162-168
    exercises (chart) 140
    front of arms (biceps) 148-152
    front of thigh (quadriceps) 179
    shoulders 180-185
    thigh 169-176
    whole body 186
weight training fitness, testing
    bench press test 20-21
    benefits of 17
    muscular fitness norms of bench press
      test 21, 21*t*
    PAR-Q questionnaire 18-19
weight training for sport
    choosing sport-specific exercises 206-207, 207*t*-211*t*
    evaluating your sport 205-206
    inserting sport-specific exercises into
      your program 207*t*-211*t*, 212
weight training programs
    benefits of 5
    muscle groups, developing 5
    success at achieving goals, determining
      5
weight training the right way
    lifting fundamentals 39-44, 40*f*-42*f*
    training with care 44-45
    warm up and cool down 45-50
weight training with aerobic exercise
    cross-training for body-shaping program
      200
    cross-training for muscle-toning program 199-200
    cross-training for strength-training program 200-201
    cross-training workout chart 204
    duration of aerobic component 203-204
    intensity of aerobic component 201-202, 202*t*, 203, 203*f*
whole body exercises, power clean (FW)
    186-187
workout-chart guidelines
    exercises, selecting and recording 28, 29
    making copies of workout chart 28
    sets and repetitions, recording 29
    training days, choosing 28, 28*t*
    workouts, locating 27
workout levels, understanding 51-53

About the Authors

Thomas R. Baechle, EdD, CSCS,*D; NSCA-CPT,*D, is the executive director of the National Strength and Conditioning Association (NSCA) Certification Commission. He is the cofounder and past president of NSCA and its former director of education. In 1985 he was named the NSCA's Strength and Conditioning Professional of the Year. Baechle is also the chair of the exercise science and athletic training department at Creighton University and the former exercise leader of their phase III cardiac rehabilitation program. He has received numerous awards, including the Lifetime Achievement Award from the NSCA and the Excellence in Teaching Award from Creighton University.

For 16 years, Baechle competed successfully in weightlifting and powerlifting, setting various Midwest records. For more than 20 years he coached collegiate powerlifting teams, strength trained athletes, and taught weight training classes. Baechle was the force behind the creation of the CSCS and NSCA-CPT examinations that are offered through the NSCA Certification Commission. In addition to *Fitness Weight Training*, Baechle has authored 10 books that have been translated into 10 languages, including the popular *Weight Training: Steps to Success*.

Roger Earle, MA, CSCS,*D; NSCA-CPT,*D, is the associate executive director and the director of exam development for the NSCA Certification Commission. He is responsible for reviewing and editing the CSCS and NSCA-CPT exams and writing study resources with Thomas Baechle, including the *Essentials of Strength Training and Conditioning* and *NSCA's Essentials of Personal Training* texts. In addition, Earle has been a personal fitness trainer for people of all ages and fitness levels for nearly 20 years.

Earle has presented at numerous national and international conferences with an emphasis on designing resistance training programs for athletes and clients of all sports and fitness levels. Before taking his position with the NSCA Certification Commission, he received his master's degree in exercise science from the University of Nebraska at Omaha. Earle's background includes nine years as a Division I strength coach and eight years as a faculty member of the exercise science and athletic training department, both at Creighton University.